Jesus Cannot Be
The Jewish Messiah*

Robert M. Pill

Book Typesetting and Cover design by Robert M. Pill
Cover Photograph by David H. Rossman. Used by permission.

ISBN: 979-8-9882917-0-1 (Hard Cover)
ISBN: 979-8-9882917-1-8 (Soft Cover)
ISBN: 979-8-9882917-2-5 (eBook)

First Edition: Year 2023 Month

10 9 8 7 6 **5** 4 3 2 1

מִשְׁלֵי כח:ט

מֵסִיר אָזְנוֹ מִשְּׁמֹעַ
תּוֹרָה גַּם־תְּפִלָּתוֹ
תּוֹעֵבָה:

Proverbs 28:9

He that turneth away his ear from hearing the Torah, even his prayer is an **abomination.**

Table of Contents

Preface

Jesus Cannot Be The Jewish Messiah!*

*I actually address this subject directly later on in this book with a chapter starting with that same statement (including the asterisk). My intention is that, at that point in the book, I will have led up to it after giving it a sufficient introduction!

Essentially, **this book is a commentary** on the man responsible for being the architect of the main doctrines of Christianity, **Saul of Tarsus,** more commonly known as **The Apostle Paul.** I have included commentaries about **Jesus of Nazareth, and the resurrection,** near the end of the book.

I also comment on **Talmudism,** the Jewish religion whose doctrine revolves around **rabbinic oral tradition.** When Talmudists mention 'Torah' **they mean the 'Oral Torah' — oral tradition! When I mention Torah, I mean the written Torah!**

I have attempted to provide salient arguments for the topics at hand, with enough supporting references and analyses to allow it to be my own way of teaching about the subjects.

Who is the intended audience? Probably, those people who have a sufficient knowledge of the Jewish Scriptures and the Christian Bible to appreciate the comparative arguments, and those who want to know and understand the implications of acknowledging the Jewish Scriptures as authoritative!

My highlighting style, herein, is often similar to a modern web page. I make certain words **bold,** ***bold-italic,*** underlined, even larger in parts to stress some of the points. Otherwise, I just use a nice san-serif font as the base font.

I realize this style is non-standard in the writing of books. However, this current generation, of whom I would like to reach, has not grown up on literature in typewritten or plain font form as much as they have from what is displayed on the internet, in web pages and even text messages on their smart phones that have more interesting highlighting of text rather than perhaps a plain, mundane typewriter font. Web pages use all sorts of visual devices to get attention or to stress points.

The Name יְהֹוָה Yehovah

You might notice that I am absolutely unafraid to write (or say) the transliterated name **Yehovah — יְהֹוָה —** in Hebrew. **Yehovah** is the transliterated **name of the God** of Abraham, Isaac and Jacob. יהוה – YHVH — the name of four letters, 'Yud' – 'Heh' – 'Vav' – 'Heh,' is also known as **the Tetragrammaton.**

יְהֹוָה — Yehovah
He Who Was, He Who Is, He Who Will Be.

The name יְהֹוָה **Yehovah** means הָיָה **'Hayah,'** *He Who Was,* הֹוֶה **'Hoveh,'** *He Who Is,* and יְהְיֶה **'Yihyeh,'** *He Who Will Be.*

If interested in knowing more about The Name יְהֹוָה – Yehovah, I refer you to the excellent resources by Dr. Nehemia Gordon found at his website: https://www.nehemiaswall.com/nehemia-gordon-name-god, or a teaching in a YouTube video which may be found at https://www.youtube.com/watch?v=YfljMUR9dKA.

Biblical Quotations

All passages from the Hebrew-language sourced Jewish Scriptures, herein, are taken from 'The Pill Tanakh: Hebrew-English Jewish Scriptures,' currently a three volume book separated into a 520 page Torah (the 5 books of Moses), 970 page Neviim (Prophets) and 688 page Ketuvim (Writings).

All passages from the Christian New Testament (Christian Bible) are taken from the King James Version (KJV).

When I reference the Jewish Scriptures, my intention is to show enough surrounding verses to provide the **contextual relevance.** Points and arguments should require the context of a reference for an accurate assessment. Thus, including enough surrounding verses to express the given context is important to intelligently express what a passage says.

I realize that some people don't read footnotes and even may skip things they may have a preconception as perhaps being mundane or unimportant. I do not wish to over-burden the reader with excessive arguments or too many references as I am aware that people, in our day, want quick answers and that they may become bored easily. **Yet, I want to be thorough!**

I apologize, in advance, if my writing style causes you consternation. However, it is my intent to be clear, though sometimes I may give what some may consider to be excessive information. I have tried to provide pertinent references so that the reader may see that I am concerned about proper context.

I have provided many references from the Jewish Scriptures as well as the Christian New Testament, not just to show the source behind the points I want to make, but also **because I realize that not everyone is familiar with those texts.**

I do want to thank you, in advance, for taking the time out of what may be a busy schedule to the reading of my work.

I am aware that the subjects, herein, may be controversial. I also realize that if one is not able to **question** cherished beliefs, **that may qualify them as to being in a *cult!***

I am of the opinion that our beliefs should always hold up to **outside scrutiny,** especially if we wish them to be considered valid by others — who may not be like-minded!

Being able to challenge our own tenets and beliefs is fundamental to having a **faith** that can be shown to be relevant beyond our own places *'where we may find a safe harbor!'*

What We Call Faith May Rather Be Fanaticism!

If our tenets and beliefs cannot be shown to be founded upon sound principles which can be backed up with relevant documentation, **then what we attribute to be faith may rather, instead, be a certain fanaticism or just plain zeal!**

Fanaticism may be founded upon sincere and strongly held beliefs, *or just upon our feelings!* However, In My Humble Opinion (**IMHO**), strongly held **beliefs and feelings** do not equal or substitute for a profound knowledge and understanding, nor should we expect them to!

I have said all of this in an effort to help you understand that, for my own views, I have tried to provide references that contain enough relevant information for a sufficient context.

It is with these sentiments that I hope you will find the reading enjoyable, and even more so that you may find it instructive and even challenging.

Blessings to all who do take the time to try to understand some of the concepts which can require a self-scrutiny that may not otherwise have been attained!

Robert Pill
September, 2023

Influence

Influence. 1. The power or capacity of causing an effect in indirect or intangible ways.[2]

The following is a <u>scenario</u> <u>regarding</u> *influence*:

> A group of books were written over the span of many decades. Each book was in some way related to the life of one man.

---

[1] Sustainable Food Trust, 'How seasonal is Easter lamb?,' last modified 28 Mar 2022, https://sustainablefoodtrust.org/news-views/how-seasonal-is-easter-lamb/. Photo Easter-Lamb-475x280.jpg converted to grayscale and image posterization applied.

[2] Merriam-Webster, `influence', https://www.merriam-webster.com/dictionary/influence, accessed 14 Jul 2022.

One particular author wrote the ***majority*** of those books. Most of his accounts appeared many decades prior to all but one of the rest of the books. The influence of the ***majority author*** was greatly enhanced as one of the remaining books was **predominantly <u>his</u> <u>own</u> <u>biography</u>**!

Suffice it to say that all of the other writers were likely familiar with this ***majority author's*** works. Their own writings could have been ***influenced by his writings.***

Over time and due to his own sphere of ***influence,*** this ***majority author*** became known as the prevailing voice of authority for ***the <u>'historical</u> <u>man</u> <u>of</u> <u>interest</u>.'*** Subsequently, in his own lifetime, he also *attributed to himself* to be the chief spokesperson of that ***'man of interest!'***

Ironically, as the story goes, the ***majority author*** and his ***'biographer author friend' <u>never</u> <u>even</u> <u>met</u> <u>the</u> <u>'man</u> <u>of</u> <u>interest!</u>'*** However, each and every one of the ***'attributed others'*** were close personal friends or relatives of that man.

The group of books were assembled into a single volume **centuries after the historical events were purported to have occurred.**

It can easily be seen that the early *majority author* could have *influenced* the thoughts and ideas in the writing of later accounts through his own writings and from the biographical account in one of the other books.

Essentially, the *majority author* could have driven the theme of expression for the later books, so that his *influence* made the *whole* to appear to have been written by a unified group, as in *one voice.*

For those of you who have __not__ 'lived __under__ a rock' much of your lives, no doubt you may surmise that the above scenario is speaking of the assembling of the **Christian New Testament** and the predominant voice *majority author* being that of the one who is known as **'The Apostle Paul.'** Paul's *'biographer friend'* was *Luke,* responsible for writing the **Gospel of Luke** and the **Book of Acts** in the Christian Bible.

Christianity has dominated and greatly influenced western culture for longer than the history of the United States of America. Our laws and institutions were founded upon principles which have long been associated with Christianity.

I want to establish that the core of Christianity's influence may be from the **religion it claims to be based upon, Judaism** — in its codification of divine law and commonly accepted instructions for righteous living. However, understanding its foundation does not necessarily lead to a healthy outlook of what it has morphed into, now far removed from its source!

The following chart is a graphic representation depicting *the potential sphere of influence* presented by showing the New

Testament books by the date of their expected year of occurrence, their authorship as well as their place of origin.

Pertinent Data on the New Testament Books

Due to the nature of the New Testament material, the matter of authorship, date, and place of origin is necessarily tentative and conjectural. Books which treat this material in a more extensive form include Feine-Behm-Kümmel, *And Introduction to the New Testament* (Protestant Liberal); D. Guthrie, *New Testament Introduction*, 3 vols. (Protestant Conservative); and A. Wikenhauser, *New Testament Introduction* (Roman Catholic). Our suggestions are as follows:

	Authorship	Date	Place of Origin
Matthew	Apostle Matthew	75-85	Antioch
Mark	John Mark	67-72	Rome
Luke	Luke	75-90	Greece?
John	Apostle John	90-100	Asia Minor
Acts	Luke	75-90	Greece?
Romans	Apostle Paul	55-56	Corinth
1 Corinthians	Paul	54-55	Ephesus
2 Corinthians	Paul	55	Macedonia
Galatians	Paul	55	Ephesus?
Ephesians	Paul	60-62	Rome
Philippians	Paul	60-62	Rome
Colossians	Paul	60-62	Rome
1 Thessalonians	Paul	50-51	Corinth
2 Thessalonians	Paul	50-51	Corinth
1 Timothy	Paul	62-64	Macedonia
2 Timothy	Paul	64-68	Rome
Titus	Paul	62-64	Macedonia
Philemon	Paul	60-62	Rome
Hebrews	Anonymous	62-66	Asia Minor?
James	James, the brother of Jesus	50-60?	Unknown
1 Peter	Apostle Peter	63-64	Rome
2 Peter	[Apostle Peter]	80-90?	Unknown
1 John	Apostle John	90-100	Asia Minor
2 John	Apostle John	90-100	Asia Minor
3 John	Apostle John	90-100	Asia Minor
Jude	Jude, the brother of Jesus	70-90?	Unknown
Revelation	Apostle John	96	Asia Minor

---

[3] Glenn W. Barker, 'The New Testament Canon', http://www.bibleresearcher.com/barker1.html, accessed 25 April 2021.

The next table shows those same books where I have placed them in their ***chronological order,*** along with some adjustments, the notes of which will follow:

Books of The Christian Scriptures
Ordered by Suspected Dates

Book	Author	Origin	Date
1 Thessalonians	Paul	Corinth	50-51
2 Thessalonians	Paul	Corinth	50-51
James	James, Jesus' Brother	Unknown	50-60?
1 Corinthians	Paul	Ephesus	54-55
2 Corinthians	Paul	Macedonia	55
Galatians	Paul	Ephesus	55
Romans	Paul	Corinth	55-56
Ephesians	Paul	Rome	60-62
Philippians	Paul	Rome	60-62
Philemon	Paul	Rome	60-62
Colossians	Paul	Rome	60-62
1 Timothy	Paul	Macedonia	62-64
Titus	Paul	Macedonia	62-64
Hebrews	Anonymous (likely Paul)	Asia Minor?	62-66
1 Peter	Sylvanus [not Peter]	Rome	63-64
John	John	Asia Minor	65*
1 John	John	Asia Minor	65*
2 John	John	Asia Minor	65*
3 John	John	Asia Minor	65*
2 Timothy	Paul	Rome	64-68
Revelation	John	Asia Minor	69*
Mark	John Mark	Rome	67-72
Matthew	Matthew	Antioch	75-85
Jude	Jude, Jesus' brother	Unknown	70-90?
Luke	Luke	Greece?	75-90
Acts	Luke	Greece?	75-90
2 Peter	[not Peter]	Unknown	> 150

* Approximated dates based upon Alfred Edersheim's observations.

Alfred Edersheim expressed that the familiar minutiae of detail of the workings of the Temple were that of a **Cohen** – a Jewish priest, found in the writings of the disciple, John. **This led Edersheim to conclude that the disciple, John, wrote his books prior to the destruction of the Temple in 70 A.D.**[4]

---

[4] Alfred Edersheim, 'The Temple: Its Ministries and Services, As They Were At The Time Of Jesus Christ', (Ira Bradley and Co., Boston, 1881), Chapter 7, pp. 112-114.

Please notice that, in this last chart, I changed the author of the book of Hebrews to '**Anonymous (likely Paul).**'

The book of **Hebrews** tells about its authorship, ending with,

> 25 'Grace be with you all. Amen. Written from Italy, by Timothy.' [Hebrews 13:25].

Yet, a different writer is inferred just **_two verses earlier:_**

> 23 'Know ye that our brother Timothy is set at liberty; with whom, if he come shortly, I will see you.' [Hebrews 13:23]

Who is the '**I**', in '**_I will see you._**'? (Hebrews 13:23) — **_can it possibly be any other than Saul of Tarsus, aka Paul?_**

Interestingly, there is a similar attribution of authorship for the book of 1st Peter:

> 12 'By Silvanus, a faithful brother unto you, as I suppose, I have written briefly, exhorting, and testifying that this is the true grace of God wherein ye stand.'
> [1 Peter 5:12]

Silvanus, who is also known as Silas, was well known as a companion of Paul in his travels.

A Book With The Highest Form Of Greek Writing

Many years ago, I found what I consider to be a great discussion on 1 & 2 Peter. That was initially found at http://www.rejectionofpascalswager.net/authorpeter.html (**now defunct**), titled, 'The Authorship of the Petrine Epistles' available, at least as of the time of this current writing, on 'The

Wayback Machine.'[5] It shows the timeline of 2nd Peter to be much later — *after the year 150 A.D.;* and, due to it having been of the **'highest form of Greek writing'** of any book of the New Testament — **to *not* possibly to have been written by a *likely* 'uneducated fisherman from the Galilee!'**

This certainly indicates that it was written at a much later time **when 'Christians' considered the writings of Paul to be 'Holy Scripture.'**[6]

That discrepancy in perceived education of one of the original Apostles should allow us to postulate that ***Peter may not have been involved at all in the writings bearing his name***!

I realize that there is an assumption that many of the attributed authors of some of the New Testament books employed scribes to record their narratives. Certainly that is a popular theory which may not be provable.

Nevertheless, it is possible that the Apostle Shimon Kefa (Simeon, Peter) could have had a Greek scribe record his books. Then, the question may be asked, ***"Did Paul use the same scribe since their books are so similar?"***

There is a general assumption that all of the books of the New Testament were originally written prior the year 100 C.E.,[7] and most actually even before the destruction of the Temple in Jerusalem in 70 C.E. The exception to that assumption is that the evangelical Christian group known as ***"premillennialists"*** would insist that the Book of The Revelation to John was written

---

[5] Paul N. Tobin, 'The Authorship of the Petrine Epistles', accessed 20 June 2012, https://web.archive.org/web/20120609021858/http://www.rejectionofpascalswager.net/authorpeter.html.

[6] Don Stewart, 'Why Are the Writings of the Apostle Paul Considered to Be Divinely Inspired,' accessed 4 May 2023, https://www.blueletterbible.org/faq/don_stewart/don_stewart_1242.cfm.

[7] Simply put, BCE (Before Common Era) is a secular version of BC (before Christ). CE (Common Era) is the secular equivalent of AD (anno Domini), which means "in the year of the Lord" in Latin. Bruce McClure, 'What is the Common Era?,' last modified 6 Nov 2020, https://earthsky.org/human-world/definition-common-era-bce-ce-bc-ad/.

sometime after 70 C.E., **likely in the 90's.** For the book of 2nd Peter, in the chronological chart I expressed for it probably to have been written after the year 150 A.D.![8]

Regarding the book of Revelation, those who insist for a late dating, as in the 90's of the common era, do so because a dating of it prior to the destruction of the Temple in Jerusalem **would destroy their creative timeline** interpretation of the book of Daniel. I will explore that later when I **briefly** discuss the evangelical Christian, end-times, premillennial viewpoint.

In the least, it is likely that Peter did not write his narratives alone. Many have remarked at the **striking similarity between 1st Peter and some of Paul's letters.**

I have included another chart, below, showing the comparison of certain verses which appear to almost be verbatim quotes found among various writings attributed to Paul!

The following chart should help to illustrate those similarities. In the least it shows what I consider to be a profound influence of the self-appointed Apostle Paul may have had on other writers!

The quotes from Paul, in the left column, are found in various books of the New Testament. The right column shows the corresponding verses in 1st Peter which are quite similar.

This side-by-side comparison certainly makes the **'voice of Peter' sound quite a bit like 'the voice of Paul!'**

See if you also agree regarding this next illustration of influence!

---

[8] Early Christian Writings, 2 Peter, 'Estimated Range of Dating: 100-160 AD,' accessed 15 February 2023, https://www.earlychristianwritings.com/2peter.html.

Eph 1:3 Praise be to the God and Father of our Lord Jesus Christ	1Pe 1:3 Praise be to the God and Father of our Lord Jesus Christ!
Col 3:8 But now you must rid yourselves of all such things as these: anger, rage, malice, slander, and filthy language from your lips.	1Pe 2:1 Therefore, rid yourselves of all malice and all deceit, hypocrisy, envy, and slander of every kind.
Eph 5:22 Wives, submit to your husbands as to the Lord.	1Pe 3:1 Wives, in the same way be submissive to your husbands
1Th 5:6 ...let us be alert and self-controlled.	1Pe 5:8 Be self-controlled and alert.
1Co 16:20 ...Greet one another with a holy kiss.	1Pe 5:14 Greet one another with a kiss of love.
Rom 8:18 ... the glory that will be revealed in us.	1Pe 5:1 ... the glory to be revealed:
Rom 4:24 ...for us who believe in him who raised Jesus our Lord from the dead.	1Pe 1:21 ... you believe in God, who raised him from the dead ...
Rom 13:1 Everyone must submit himself to the governing authorities...	Pe 2:13 Submit yourselves for the Lord's sake to every authority instituted among men
Rom 12:6 We have different gifts, according to the grace given us. If a man's gift is prophesying, let him use it in proportion to his faith. Rom 12:7 If it is serving, let him serve; if it is teaching, let him teach;	1Pe 4:10 Each one should use whatever gift he has received to serve others, faithfully administering God's grace in its various forms. 1Pe 4:11 If anyone speaks, he should do it as one speaking the very words of God. If anyone serves, he should do it with the strength God provides
1Ti 2:9 I also want women to dress modestly, with decency and propriety, not with braided hair or gold or pearls or expensive clothes,	1Pe 3:3 Your beauty should not come from outward adornment, such as braided hair and the wearing of gold jewelry and fine clothes.

9

A summary from the same source as above adds more information for the point of this discussion:

Beyond the similarity of many verses of Paul and Peter, the overall structure of his plea is

9 Christian Unity, '1 Peter: Paul, Silas, and Peter', Last modified August 25, 2009, https://christianunityblog.net/2009/08/25/1-peter-paul-silas-and-peter/

the same. Peter introduced the letter by identifying himself as an apostle. He proceeded to identify his intended audience by their location and by the blessings they have received from God. He extends grace and peace. Next he describes in more detail the great blessings they have received from God. Then he proceeds to call for an appropriate response to those blessings. This is all very – Pauline — compare to Ephesians, Colossians, and Romans. However, Peter seems to go back and forth several times — lavish description of blessings, then calling for a response, then revisiting the blessings, and calling for a response again, etc.

Overall, the similarity to Paul's letters is unmistakable. And there is a good reason for that similarity. 1 Pet 5:12 tells us that Peter wrote this letter with the help of Silas (Gk Silvanus). There is virtually unanimous agreement that this is the same Silas who accompanied Paul on his second missionary journey (approximately AD 51-54.) ...[10]

Again, I believe that the above comparison shows the potential influence that the **self-appointed Apostle Paul** had on later writers of the books that became part of the New Testament, aka 'the New Covenant' and 'the Christian Bible!'

Not Written In Israel?

In addition to the predominance of Paul's writings among the books of the Christian Bible, it should be noted that, in spite of the purported history having been set within the land of Israel,

---

[10] ibid.

absolutely *none of the books are presumed, by many, to have been written in the land of Israel itself!*

Should I also suggest, then, that writers for the majority of the books of the Christian New Testament may not have been native-born Israelites, i.e. Jews, but rather Gentiles identifying themselves by the attributed author's names?

Again, the chronological timeline chart, above, shows a possible time order of the New Testament books. It clearly indicates that only one other author, James, may have written after Paul's books to the Thessalonians, but prior to Paul's remaining accounts. Also, it shows that only one of Paul's books, 2nd Timothy, followed any other author's books!

A person may actually be found *'living under that rock'* who still thinks that Paul had little or no influence on the other authors of the books of the New Testament!

Moreover, I do not wish to presume that all readers will recognize that the **historical man of interest** mentioned above is anyone other than the man known as **Jesus of Nazareth!**

It is to **Jesus of Nazareth** that the Christian New Testament regards as *'the man of interest!'*

Quite interesting is that *world history* has actually been altered by just the knowledge of the life of the man known as **Jesus** (יֵשׁוּעַ – the name in Hebrew, transliterated as 'Yeshua').

For an example, the Gregorian calendar expresses world **calendar time to be based upon the expected year of Jesus's birth!** As a matter of fact, it has attributed the term 'B.C.' (Before Christ) to dates before the birth of Jesus.[11]

---

[11] In English, it is common for "A.D." to precede the year, so that the translation of "A.D. 2022" would read "in the year of our lord 2022." In recent years, an alternative form of B.C./A.D. has

According to the books of the New Testament, the life of Jesus took place entirely in the land of Israel, with the exception of a short time he is said to have spent, just after birth, in the land of Egypt. New Testament writers express Jesus to have lived to be thirty-three years old when he was executed by the Roman army, which was at that time policing Jerusalem, Israel.

An uninformed, casual observer may rightly ask, **"Why is there such an interest in the life of this one man?"**

No doubt but **the answer is quite complex.** In essence, the Christian New Testament writers are **convinced that *Jesus of Nazareth is 'the long expected Jewish Messiah*!'**

In my opinion, Christian writers attempted to authenticate their ideas about *'the Jewish Messiah'* by selectively choosing *incomplete* **snippets of passages from what they considered to be the authoritative Jewish Scriptures.**

Since they quoted snippets from the Jewish Scriptures, no doubt they easily could have shown the full contexts of their sources. Yet, as it turns out, they quite obviously did not!

Moreover, it appears that many *'so-called Bible believers'* of our day **rarely** look to the Hebrew-language based Jewish Scriptures to verify what has been presented as authoritative

---

gained traction. Many publications use "C.E.," or "common era," and "B.C.E.," or "before common era" in order to make non-Christians more comfortable using the system. Before we talk about how and why the system was invented, let's get some historical context.
In the early Middle Ages, the most important calculation, and thus one of the main motivations for the European study of mathematics, was the problem of when to celebrate Easter. The First Council of Nicaea, in A.D. 325, had decided that Easter would fall on the Sunday following the full moon that follows the spring equinox. Computus (Latin for computation) was the procedure for calculating this most important date, and the computations were set forth in documents known as Easter tables. It was on one such table that, in A.D. 525, a monk named Dionysius Exiguus (sometimes called Dennis the Small) of Scythia Minor introduced the A.D. system, counting the years since the birth of Christ wrote Georges Declercq, a history instructor at Vrije Universiteit Brussel in an article published in the 2002 edition of the journal Sacris Erudiri.
Owen Jarus and Robert Coolman, 'Keeping time: The origin of B.C. and A.D.,' published 14 Jan 2022, https://www.livescience.com/45510-anno-domini.html.

references. I also find it quite curious that so many of those same people typically refer to the Jewish Scriptures as 'the **old Testament**' or 'the **old** Covenant!'

The real **travesty** I see from that viewpoint is that, **_if it has been presumed_** that the Jewish Scriptures were given by Yehovah, the Almighty-Creator-Elohim, aka God, _then to discard them, treat them with disrespect **and even call them 'old'** is not just **arrogant,** but it shows a **certain lack of respect for the Almighty, the Creator – God!** Another way of saying this, it is just plain wrong — **essentially calling what The Creator Elohim-God has declared as 'HOLY' to be common, profane, old, outdated or simply _done-away-with!_**

By merely referencing selective snippets of passages from the Jewish Scriptures as the basis for their authority, could those authors/scribes, of the New Testament, have posited a presumption that the **_idea of the Messiah_** was prominently on the hearts and minds of the majority of Israelites around the time of those occurrences?

Is that an established fact or merely an **_assumption_** put forth in the written narratives themselves? Moreover, were **_selective portions of passages from the Jewish Scriptures_** taken within their naturally occurring contexts and presented in an interpretation just as the native Israelite, Jewish, people would have done at the time of the first century of the common era?

Did New Testament writers have a **_Jewish ethos of understanding regarding the authority of the Jewish Scripture_** as it was interpreted by first century native Israelites?

To repeat, it appears that most, if not all, of the New Testament books may have been **_authored outside of the land of Israel!_** In my opinion, New Testament writers all start from a standpoint that the idea of a **central Messiah** figure was at the forefront of most every Jewish mind at the time of Jesus.

Moreover, there appears to be a prevalent presumption among 'adherents' that when the Jewish Scripture is quoted, it is fully understood to be 'true and in context' in the source document.

I personally do not believe that the idea for an immediacy of the coming of a central Messiah figure *was part of the social fabric in the life of Israelites in the first century of the common era!*

What, you may ask, *'Are you trying to rewrite history?'*

Actually, I am also trying to understand it! However, I certainly do not want to be accused of wearing *'rose colored glasses!'*

I do not believe that *there is objective, compelling evidence* that there was a prevailing sense of the urgency and immediacy for the coming of **the Jewish Messiah** among the Jewish people at the time of the life of Jesus in the first century!

Moreover, the prevalent Jewish authorities at that time were **Pharisees,** who easily could be said to be the **progenitors of Talmudic Judaism, the emergent religion based upon rabbinic discourses** – mostly unwritten – rather than the written Hebrew-language based Jewish Scriptures!

I believe that **any ideas for the advent of the Messiah would have been presumed by 'Christians' at a much later time.** Of course, **that idea may have been promulgated** from a little story found written **by Paul's biographer friend, Luke:**

> 21   And   when   eight   days   were accomplished for the circumcising of the child, his name was called JESUS, which was so named of the angel before he was conceived in the womb.

22 And when the days of her purification according to the law of Moses were accomplished, they brought him to Jerusalem, to present him to the Lord;

23 (As it is written in the law of the Lord, Every male that openeth the womb shall be called holy to the Lord;)

24 And to offer a sacrifice according to that which is said in the law of the Lord, A pair of turtledoves, or two young pigeons.

25 And, behold, there was a man in Jerusalem, whose name was Simeon; and the same man was just and devout, waiting for the consolation of Israel: and the Holy Ghost was upon him.

26 And it was revealed unto him by the Holy Ghost, that he should not see death, before he had seen the Lord's Christ.

27 And he came by the Spirit into the temple: and when the parents brought in the child Jesus, to do for him after the custom of the law,

28 Then took he him up in his arms, and blessed God, and said,

29 Lord, now lettest thou thy servant depart in peace, according to thy word:

30 For mine eyes have seen thy salvation,

31 Which thou hast prepared before the face of all people;

32 A light to lighten the Gentiles, and the glory of thy people Israel.

³³ And Joseph and his mother marvelled at those things which were spoken of him.

³⁴ And Simeon blessed them, and said unto Mary his mother, Behold, this child is set for the fall and rising again of many in Israel; and for a sign which shall be spoken against;

³⁵ (Yea, a sword shall pierce through thy own soul also,) that the thoughts of many hearts may be revealed.

³⁶ And there was one Anna, a prophetess, the daughter of Phanuel, of the tribe of Aser: she was of a great age, and had lived with an husband seven years from her virginity;

³⁷ And she was a widow of about fourscore and four years, which departed not from the temple, but served God with fastings and prayers night and day.

³⁸ And she coming in that instant gave thanks likewise unto the Lord, and spake of him to all them that looked for redemption in Jerusalem. [Luke 2:21-38]

The stories of Simeon and Anna are not found in any other New Testament book. Yet, their inclusion in the Gospel of Luke certainly gives an impression that there was a prevalent expectation among the Jewish people of a coming Messiah!

As intimated earlier, I actually do not believe that there was much Jewish thought regarding Messiah until over a millennium later when the world was dominated by an Roman Catholic, 'Christian,' ethos, which was already centered around the *idea of the man Jesus being known as 'the Jewish Messiah.'*

I am also of the opinion that it was only after many centuries of **'Roman Catholic Rule'** and **persecutions** into the early middle ages which spawned what actually became a *polemic against Christianity* **by Jewish authorities.**

In our modern age, knowledge of that animosity between religions makes it appear that polemic began with the advent of the Christian religion, rather than at a much later time.

The writings, from the early middle ages, of prominent rabbis such as Maimonides and Rashi,[12] helped foment that polemic against the authoritative religious dominance of the Roman Catholic Church, which certainly executed its autocratic rule through sympathetic governmental institutions.

As I understand it, the Roman Catholic Church dominated world governments after the third century C.E.[13] This dominance began under the Roman Emperor Constantine. **A successor,**

---

[12] 'Perhaps the greatest of our post-biblical scholars was the renowned Aristotelian philosopher and physician to the Sultan of Egypt, Rabbi Moses ben Maimon, commonly known as the Rambam or Maimonides.

'Born in Cordova, Spain he fled to Fostat, Egypt in the 12th century and there he created his masterpieces of Jewish law. He compiled all the laws of the Torah and Talmud and assembled them into one single volume, written in clear Hebrew for all to read and understand.

'900 years later, the Mishneh Torah of Maimonides remains the primary text of Jewish religious law. Written over a period of ten years from 1170-1180, it included the Taryag Mitzvot, the 613 divine commandments which are required to be observed by every Jew.'

'The greatest of the Bible and Talmud commentators, Rabbi Shlomo Yitzchaki (Rashi) was born in Troyes, France and witnessed the massacre of Jews by the Crusaders en route to the Holy Land. His commentaries on the Bible and Talmud have been required study of every Jewish student in yeshivot from the 11th century to the present day. No Hebrew Bible is printed without Rashi's explanation underneath the Hebrew text. He is held by religious Jews everywhere as the greatest commentator and interpreter of the Hebrew Bible and Talmud.'

'Unlike Rambam, Rashi was not a philosopher nor a physician. He was a vinoculturist by trade and one of the most recognized Jewish scholars over the many long centuries.'

Esor Ben-Sorek, The Times of Israel, 'Rambam and Rashi, the Greatest Among the Great,' https://blogs.timesofisrael.com/rambam-and-rashi-the-greatest-among-the-great/,last modified 7 June 2018.

[13] J.F. Matthews and Donald MacGillivray Nicol, 'Constantine I Roman emperor,' last updated 29 Mar 2023, https://www.britannica.com/biography/Constantine-I-Roman-emperor.

Theodosius 1, declared the 'then version of Christianity' to be the official state religion of the Roman Empire.[14]

I am also of the opinion that the Roman Catholic Church probably rewrote much of early history regarding the foundation of Christianity, and also destroyed or hid essential manuscripts, which, if known, may have been detrimental to its system of beliefs.

Maimonides is attributed to having written the following quote:

אני מאמין באמונה שלמה בביאת
המשיח: ואף על פי שיתמהמה עם
כל־זה אחכה־לו כל־יום שיבוא:

'I believe with perfect faith in the coming of the Moshiach. Though he tarry, nonetheless, I will await him every day, that he will come.'[15]

So, the **idea of Messiah** was at least part of the Jewish ethos at the time of Maimonides, who lived in the 12th century C.E.

Again, this way of thinking does not seem to have been occurring prominently among the Jewish people until the middle ages following the writings of Rashi and Maimonides!

---

[14] Matthias von Hellfeld, 'Christianity becomes the religion of the Roman Empire - February 27, 380,' last updated 16 Nov 2009, https://www.dw.com/en/christianity-becomes-the-religion-of-the-roman-empire-february-27-380/a-4602728.

[15] Mishnah Sanhedrin, Chapter 10, Principle 12. Part of the thirteen foundations of Jewish {i.e. Torah} Faith compiled by Rabbi Moses ben Maimon (1135-1204 C.E.; also known as Maimonides). He is referred to by the acronym for his name, which is Rambam. Rambam wrote the thirteen foundations in his Commentary on the Mishnah, in the tenth chapter of Tractate Sanhedrin. He wrote this in Arabic while he was living in Egypt. It was later translated into Hebrew... U.N.A. Course: Foundations of Torah, Principles of Faith, and Moshiach (the Messiah), https://asknoah.org/wp-content/uploads/UNA-Class2-Lesson1.pdf, modified 2011.

Getting back to the first century of the common era, there was a Jewish-born historian for the Roman Empire, known to us as **Josephus**. His writings appeared sometime after the Roman army's destruction of the Temple in Jerusalem in 70 A.D.

Like so many ancient writings, **_many scholars consider that his writings suffered corruption at the hands of zealous scribes,_** particularly those appearing after the Roman Empire became transformed into a religious institution.

Nonetheless, it appears that in and around 93-94 AD, Josephus' writings may have mentioned **Jesus of Nazareth** actually centering around his brother, James. However, **those references are quite debatable as to have occurred at all;** early references to Josephus may prove spurious at best.[16]

In the least, there are absolutely **no references regarding 'The Apostle Paul' in ancient historical** _accounts outside of Christian writings,_ **including those of Josephus.**

Quite obviously, it is not easy to reconstruct the now ancient history of early Christianity from non-Christian and supposedly neutral or **_objective_** sources.

That is one of the reasons I wanted to show the potential influence of the most prolific author of early Christianity, which I believe is further substantiated from the chronological ordering of New Testament books. In fact, by my chronological table, I have shown that Paul and Luke may be responsible for writing sixteen of the twenty-seven books of the New Testament!

Defining The Past
Based Upon Our Perceptions Of The Present

---

16 Richard Carrier, 'Josephus on Jesus? Why You Can't Cite Opinions Before 2014', https://www.richardcarrier.info/archives/12071, last modified 15 February 2017.

It is imperitive that we do not fall into the _trap_ of defining the past based upon our perceptions of the present!

I am hopeful that I made a proper case of how the earliest New Testament writings could have influenced the later ones. We must base our understanding of the past from what we can glean from the history that is available to us at the present.

It certainly appears that world history and Christian history have been intertwined since Christianity became the state religion of the Roman Empire following Emperor Constantine.

How about another **'wrinkle into the mix?'**

The following quote is probably a fairly common viewpoint regarding the expected source for New Testament quotes of the _presumptive_ Jewish Scriptures:

> 'Yes, the proper understanding of Scripture is a game changer (as it should be).'
>
> 'Of the multitude of Old Testament quotes in the New Testament, most of them came from the Septuagint (abbreviated LXX – the Greek translation of the Old Testament). This translation of the Old Testament is the oldest in existence, was widely used by the Apostles and all Jews at the time of Christ, and included the so–called 'apocryphal' or 'deuterocanonical' books that Protestants later removed.'[17]

Yet, at least one author has a view of the Septuagint quite different than the prevailing views of its ancient origins!

---

[17] Fr. John A. Peck, 'Septuagint Quotes in the New Testament,' Preacher' Institute,' last modified 21 Aug 2019, https://preachersinstitute.com/2019/08/21/septuagint-quotes-in-thenew-testament/.

The <u>Legend</u> Of An Ancient Greek Old Testament

I mention this author and quote from his book because, **unlike others, _he actually does a thorough job of documenting his beliefs_.** A sampling of those views are as follows:

> 'When we trace back through the Alexandrian (southern) stream of Bible manuscripts, we find the legend of a Greek Old Testament called the 'Septuagint.' Scholars like to say it was made about 285 BC. But, like most of the other documents in this polluted stream, once you ask some basic questions, you start to doubt the official story of its age —and of its being 'oldest and best.'

> 'But what if I could show you where the Greek Old Testament, that they call the 'Septuagint,' supposedly written in 285 BC, copied 48 words in a row from the Apostle Paul's letter to the Romans (57-58 AD), into the Psalms, which David originally wrote 1,000 years earlier?'

> 'I know that was a complex sentence. But please realize this. Trying to explain the creation of the Septuagint Greek Old Testament is like trying to eat an elephant. So let me take this just one tiny bite at a time.'

'Why is this important? Because remember, this supposedly '285 BC' Greek Old Testament, called the Septuagint, has been said by Roman Catholics and other professors to have more authority than the Hebrew, because they say it was the Bible used by Jesus and the apostles!'

'Because of that, Roman Catholics said it was inspired. Then they took that 'Septuagint' Greek Old Testament and had it translated into Latin. That Latin became the Old Testament of the Roman Catholic Latin Vulgate. And that Roman Catholic Latin Vulgate was later translated by Jesuits into an English Bible in 1582-1610 and called the Douay-Rheims Bible. ...'

'The Catholic Bible didn't go back to the Hebrew. It only went back to the 'Septuagint' Greek Old Testament.'[18]

Moreover, David Daniels expressed that the Septuagint is more likely to have been written at a much later time than many others have suggested. He dates it after the year 300 A.D.

This could also affect our understanding regarding the New Testament writings, because, as can be discerned, a full two

---

[18] David W. Daniels, 'Did Jesus Use The Septuagint' (Ontario, CA, Chick Publications), pp 12, 15, 16. Reproduced by permission.
See link to David Daniels' video series, 'Was There A B.C. Septuagint?,' https://youtube.com/playlist?list=PLhmAbEGx-AnRh2YgrQvayYIEItaAoISWA (playlist); a link can also be found at https://www.the-iconoclast.org/resources/.

thirds of the references purported to be from the Jewish Scriptures are actually taken from the Greek Septuagint!

It is my understanding that David Daniels, in addition to his analysis of what has been considered to be actual historical evidence, may also have based his late dating of the Septuagint upon his discovery of 48 words in a row found in one of the Psalms of David, which were actually a direct copy, from the book of Romans, of the words of Saul of Tarsus, known to Christians as the Apostle Paul.

Forty-eight (48) contiguous words in the Psalms found in the Septuagint <u>were</u> <u>the</u> <u>exact</u> <u>same</u> <u>Greek</u> <u>words</u> <u>that</u> <u>Paul</u> <u>wrote</u> <u>in</u> <u>the</u> <u>book</u> <u>of</u> <u>Romans</u>! It should be rather obvious that those words in the Septuagint, for the Psalms, were <u>not</u> from in the Hebrew-language based Jewish Scriptures!

Is there also a possibility that the Septuagint could have used the Greek Christian New Testament as the source for its over 200 quotes from the "presumptive Jewish Scriptures?"

So, how much influence did the Greek Septuagint have on the Christian New Testament?

> 'Of the approximately 300 Old Testament quotes in the New Testament, approximately 2/3 of them came from the Septuagint (the Greek translation of the Old Testament) which included the deuterocanonical books that the Protestants later removed. This is additional evidence that Jesus and the apostles viewed the deuterocanonical books as part of canon of the Old Testament.'[19]

Two Thirds! Two–thirds of the quotes from what Christians call the 'Old Testament' (how most refer to the Jewish Scriptures)

---

[19] Scripture Catholic, 'SEPTUAGINT QUOTES IN THE NEW TESTAMENT,' accessed 3 Oct 2022, https://www.scripturecatholic.com/septuagint-quotes-new-testament/.

certainly indicates a significant influence in and of itself. That alone presents the possibility of a huge problem in understanding *but also of it potentially being spurious!*

Further, by quoting two-thirds of the presumptive 'Jewish Scriptures' from **the potentially later, *modern* 'Greek Old Testament'** known as the Septuagint, the actual authorship and/or editing-completion of New Testament books may have occurred sometime after the Roman Catholic Church came into being! **You may have heard that *winners rewrite history!***

It is understood that the Roman Emperors, beginning with Constantine, acknowledged **'the then-version-of-Christianity'** to be the state religion of the Roman Empire!

With that as a backdrop, I want to conclude with another *'wrinkle into the mix,'* if you will allow me the license to do so!

Regarding the writing and then the potential of a much later assembling of the books of the New Testament, I believe there is quite a **possibility that *history itself has been rewritten!***

What If *Satan* Rewrote The History?

If an entity known as **'Satan'** exists, is it possible that he could have **stolen the narratives** about the true Messiah *and made a new story more acceptable to the gullible masses?*

Along the same lines, another question might be, "If the entity known as **'Satan'** exists, then was his power held in check from interfering with the knowledge and history of the life of Jesus, and also while the New Testament was being assembled?"

In Christian circles, the subject is covered in many places and uses passages from both the Jewish Scriptures as well as the

Christian New Testament to describe the idea.[20] Many of those sources have given references to some of the more well known passages.[21]

Essentially, to construe an idea of a **ha-Satan** (the Satan), a nefarious being devoted to the destruction of mankind, is not all that unusual; it is found in many other religions as well.[22]

However, in much of **Jewish thinking,** passages such as found in Isaiah 45 *often seem to attribute all causation, good as well as evil, to Yehovah (God) alone.*

---

[20] Stephen Flurry, 'Who Is the God of This World? And how will his rule come to an end?,' the Trumpet, August 2010, https://www.thetrumpet.com/7301-who-is-the-god-of-this-world.

[21] Isaiah 14:12: How art thou fallen from heaven, O day-star, son of the morning! How art thou cut down to the ground, that didst cast lots over the nations!

Ezekiel 28:14: Thou wast the far-covering cherub; and I set thee, so that thou wast upon the holy mountain of God; thou hast walked up and down in the midst of stones of fire.

Matthew 4:1-11: Then was Jesus led up of the Spirit into the wilderness to be tempted of the devil.

[2] And when he had fasted forty days and forty nights, he was afterward an hungred.

[3] And when the tempter came to him, he said, If thou be the Son of God, command that these stones be made bread.

[4] But he answered and said, It is written, Man shall not live by bread alone, but by every word that proceedeth out of the mouth of God.

[5] Then the devil taketh him up into the holy city, and setteth him on a pinnacle of the temple,

[6] And saith unto him, If thou be the Son of God, cast thyself down: for it is written, He shall give his angels charge concerning thee: and in their hands they shall bear thee up, lest at any time thou dash thy foot against a stone.

[7] Jesus said unto him, It is written again, Thou shalt not tempt the Lord thy God.

[8] Again, the devil taketh him up into an exceeding high mountain, and sheweth him all the kingdoms of the world, and the glory of them;

[9] And saith unto him, All these things will I give thee, if thou wilt fall down and worship me.

[10] Then saith Jesus unto him, Get thee hence, Satan: for it is written, Thou shalt worship the Lord thy God, and him only shalt thou serve.

[11] Then the devil leaveth him, and, behold, angels came and ministered unto him.

John 12:1 : Now is the judgment of this world: now shall the prince of this world be cast out.

John 14:30 : Hereafter I will not talk much with you: for the prince of this world cometh, and hath nothing in me.

2 Corinthians 4:4 : In whom the god of this world hath blinded the minds of them which believe not, lest the light of the glorious gospel of Christ, who is the image of God, should shine unto them.

Ephesians 2:2 : Wherein in time past ye walked according to the course of this world, according to the prince of the power of the air, the spirit that now worketh in the children of disobedience:

Revelation 12:9: And the great dragon was cast out, that old serpent, called the Devil, and Satan, which deceiveth the whole world: he was cast out into the earth, and his angels were cast out with him.

[22] Britannica, 'Varieties of angels and demons in the religions of the world,' accessed 31 Mar 2023, https://www.britannica.com/topic/angel-religion/Varieties-of-angels-and-demons-in-the-religions-of-the-world.

5 I am Yehovah, and there is none else, beside Me there is no God; I have girded thee, though thou hast not known Me; I am Yehovah, and there is none else, beside Me there is no God; I have girded thee, though thou hast not known Me;

6 That they may know from the rising of the sun, and from the west, that there is none beside Me; I am Yehovah; and there is none else;

7 I form the light, and create darkness; I make peace, and create evil; I am Yehovah, that doeth all these things. [Isaiah 45:5-7]

Isaiah 45:7 is often quoted in modern Jewish circles to express the idea that there is only one heavenly being who creates both the good and the evil; and that being is Almighty God alone!

Obviously, that thinking could negate the idea of there even being *angels* as well! Thus, Isaiah 45:7 should probably not be the basis for a proof text to posit the idea of there not being such a being as ha-Satan. In fact, there is a passage in the second chapter of the book of Job which mentions **Satan** by name!

1 Again it fell upon a day, that the sons of God came to present themselves before Yehovah, and Satan came also among them to present himself before Yehovah.

2 And Yehovah said unto Satan: 'From whence comest thou?' And Satan

answered Yehovah, and said: 'From going to and fro in the earth, and from walking up and down in it.'

³ And Yehovah said unto Satan: 'Hast thou considered my servant Job, that there is none like him in the earth, a whole-hearted and an upright man, one that feareth God, and shunneth evil? and he still holdeth fast his integrity, although thou didst move Me against him, to destroy him without cause.'

⁴ And Satan answered Yehovah, and said: 'Skin for skin, yea, all that a man hath will he give for his life.

⁵ But put forth Thy hand now, and touch his bone and his flesh, surely he will blaspheme Thee to Thy face.'

⁶ And Yehovah said unto Satan: 'Behold, he is in thy hand; only spare his life.'

⁷ So Satan went forth from the presence of Yehovah, and smote Job with sore boils from the sole of his foot even unto his crown. [Job 2:1-7]

This certainly does not exhaust the subject, but I believe it does provide some references useful in understanding it.

The idea of the history of Christianity, defined in the Christian Scriptures, as **being untouched by nefarious entities, whether angelic or human, is probably a bit naive.** In fact ['putting words in their mouths'], it is like they would argue, *"Satan exists, but he was unable to interfere with the Christian message because our Jesus and our Paul prevented him!"*

My intention has been to provide a sense of the great influence that Saul of Tarsus ('the Apostle Paul') had on the **foundation** and **doctrines** of the Christian religion, which has profoundly influenced much of the English–Speaking Western World.

Moreover, I wanted to establish the **potential of a rewriting of Christian and World history** by the Roman Catholic Church, especially after the time that the Roman Emperor, Theodosius 1, made 'Christianity' the **state religion** of the Roman Empire.

The likelihood of a much later dating for the New Testament books may be surmised by the fact that a full two thirds of the written quotations of the presumed Jewish Scriptures were taken from the Greek Septuagint. Again, David Daniels dates the Septuagint to sometime **after the year 300 A.D.**

I believe that statement lends credence to my accusation of the *Roman Catholic Church as having **rewritten** the early history of Christianity,* effectively making **Paul the <u>proxy</u> Messiah through the influence of writings attributed to him.** Paul clearly authored over half of the New Testament.

To try to say that the self-appointed Apostle Paul had little or no influence on later writers is a bit naive, IMHO!

Influence. 1. The power or capacity of causing an effect in indirect or intangible ways.[23]

---

[23] Merriam-Webster, `influence', https://www.merriam-webster.com/dictionary/influence, accessed 14 Jul 2022.

The False Prophet

24

¹⁵ **Beware of false prophets, which come to you in sheep's clothing, but inwardly they are ravening wolves.** [Matt. 7:15]

⁴ **And Jesus answered and said unto them, Take heed that no man deceive you.**
⁵ **For many shall come in my name, saying, I am Christ; and shall deceive many.** [Matt. 24:4-5]

¹ **All this word which I command you, that shall ye observe to do; thou shalt not add thereto, nor diminish from it.**
² **If there arise in the midst of thee a prophet, or a dreamer of dreams--and he give thee a sign or a wonder,**
³ **and the sign or the wonder come to pass, whereof he spoke unto thee--**

---

²⁴ Shravasti Dhammika, 'Wolves In Sheep's Clothing,' dhamma musings, last modified 4 Jan 2012, https://sdhammika.blogspot.com/2012/01/wolves-in-sheeps-clothing.html. Photo wolf[1].jpg converted to grayscale, feathered fleece into wolf, image posterization applied.

saying: 'Let us go after other gods, which thou hast not known, and let us serve them';

4 thou shalt not hearken unto the words of that prophet, or unto that dreamer of dreams; for Yehovah your God putteth you to proof, to know whether ye do love Yehovah your God with all your heart and with all your soul.

5 After Yehovah your God shall ye walk, and Him shall ye fear, and His commandments shall ye keep, and unto His voice shall ye hearken, and Him shall ye serve, and unto Him shall ye cleave.

6 And that prophet, or that dreamer of dreams, shall be put to death; because he hath spoken perversion against Yehovah your God, who brought you out of the land of Egypt, and redeemed thee out of the house of bondage, to draw thee aside out of the way which Yehovah thy God commanded thee to walk in. So shalt thou put away the evil from the midst of thee. [Deuteronomy 13:1-6]

20 But the prophet, that shall speak a word presumptuously in My name, which I have not commanded him to speak, or that shall speak in the name of other gods, that same prophet shall die.

²¹ And if thou say in thy heart: 'How shall we know the word which Yehovah hath not spoken?'
²² When a prophet speaketh in the name of Yehovah, if the thing follow not, nor come to pass, that is the thing which Yehovah hath not spoken; the prophet hath spoken it presumptuously, thou shalt not be afraid of him.
[Deuteronomy 18:20-22]

Question: *How many false prophecies* does a person have to give in order to be declared a *false prophet?*

Answer: It only takes **One False Prophecy** to declare a *'so–called prophet'* as a *False Prophet!*

1 FALSE PROPHECY == 1 FALSE PROPHET!

Did Saul of Tarsus, aka 'The Apostle Paul,' ever give a prophecy that was false, i.e., which was never fulfilled?

YES!

²³ For there stood by me this night the angel of God, whose I am, and whom I serve,
²⁴ Saying, Fear not, Paul; thou must be brought before Caesar: and, lo, God hath given thee all them that sail with thee.
[Acts 27:23-24]

According to this purported vision, *this prophetic utterance,* Paul said that he was told that **he would be brought before**

Caesar and no passengers would be lost *("... God hath given thee all them that sail with thee." - Acts 27:24b).*

Ironically, Paul's friend, ***Luke, devoted over a chapter to showing the fulfillment of the last part of Paul's prophecy!***

He was emphatically clear that the latter part of Paul's vision came to pass, summed up in the following verse:

> [44] And the rest, some on boards, and some on broken pieces of the ship. And so it came to pass, that they escaped all safe to land. [Acts 27:44]

It seems rather **disingenuous** that *Luke was strangely silent* in regards to giving a description of the fulfillment of the first part of Paul's prophecy — that he would be brought before Caesar.[25]

Again, Luke was extremely descriptive in detailing the part of the prophecy regarding the lives of the people on board the ship, **devoting over a chapter to expressing its fulfillment!**[26]

Since he gave such an informative account of all that happened on the storm–tossed ship *where Paul had given his prophetic utterance,* **Luke provided absolutely no detail for the fulfillment of the first part of Paul's vision!**

Almost in passing, he made mention that Paul was in Rome for two years.[27] The following are the last two verses of the book of Acts, which provide the only recorded detail of the end of Paul's time in Rome:

---

[25] Acts 27:23-24 [23] For there stood by me this night the angel of God, whose I am, and whom I serve, [24] Saying, Fear not, Paul; thou must be brought before Caesar: and, lo, God hath given thee all them that sail with thee.
[26] see Acts, Chapters 27 & 28.
[27] Acts 28:30 [30] And Paul dwelt two whole years in his own hired house, and received all that came in unto him,

³⁰ And Paul dwelt two whole years in his own hired house, and received all that came in unto him,

³¹ Preaching the kingdom of God, and teaching those things which concern the Lord Jesus Christ, with all confidence, no man forbidding him. [Acts 28:30-31]

Moreover, I find it rather dubious that a *'supposed angel of the most high God'* addressed the 'self–proclaimed <u>Jew</u>,' Saul of Tarsus, as **Paul,** at that time an obviously non-Jewish name!'

This man, Paul, elsewhere pronounced of himself that he was *'a Hebrew of the Hebrews;'²⁸* which is, in the least, easily interpreted as a declaration of genuine Jewish ethnicity.

I must ask, *"Why would an angel of the Most High God address the Jewish Saul by his Greek, Gentile Christian name, Paul"* — <u>instead</u> of <u>his</u> supposedly <u>Hebrew</u> <u>given name,</u> <u>Saul,</u> *<u>in</u> <u>his</u> supposedly <u>native tongue,</u> <u>Hebrew</u>*?

The Most Excellent 'Theophilus'

Further, Luke was clear and emphatic in the preamble of both of the books attributed to him, **Luke** and **Acts**, where he directed his methodology in seeking the truth to a 'Theophilus':

¹ 'Forasmuch as many have taken in hand to set forth in order a declaration of those things which are most surely believed among us,'

---

²⁸ Philippians 3:5 Circumcised the eighth day, of the stock of Israel, of the tribe of Benjamin, an Hebrew of the Hebrews; as touching the law, a Pharisee;

2 'Even as they delivered them unto us, which from the beginning were eyewitnesses, and ministers of the word;'

3 'It seemed good to me also, having had perfect understanding of all things from the very first, to write unto thee in order, most excellent Theophilus,'

4 'That thou mightest know the certainty of those things, wherein thou hast been instructed.' [Luke 1:1-4]

1 'The former treatise have I made, O Theophilus, of all that Jesus began both to do and teach,'

2 'Until the day in which he was taken up, after that he through the Holy Ghost had given commandments unto the apostles whom he had chosen:' [Acts 1:1-2]

Why do I think this is important?

Because it appears that there is **no actual** 'hard evidence' which establishes, beyond a reasonable doubt, that 'Saul of Tarsus' (aka Paul) **ever actually faced Caesar** — as he had emphatically and clearly **prophesied on the ship which was, in fact, on the sea for the purpose of sailing to Rome!**

If Paul DID NOT actually face Caesar, *he is clearly a false prophet!*

In searching out whether or not Paul appeared before Caesar, I was only able to find *'circular arguments.'* I was unable to find any conclusive, objective evidence of prophetic fulfillment.

The **main 'proof'** given by **Christian apologists** is actually based upon **'_a church tradition_'** provided by the writings of so-called '**church fathers**,' which basically states that **'_Paul was beheaded at the hands of Caesar Nero._'**

Otherwise, most other **'_apologies_'** fall into a singular category, which argues that the proof is in the text itself.[29] Essentially, that argument is, "Because the prophecy is in the text of the '_**Holy Scriptures**,_' the resulting event is inherent, absolute truth!"

Of course, that presumption is based upon the idea that all of the New Testament is considered to be '**sacred, Holy Scripture**,' and, as such may not be questioned nor challenged.

Essentially, the argument is that because Paul said it, it must be true — Paul's prophecy had to have occurred simply because 'the Christian Scripture' records the declaration itself!

Again, Luke's account is completely silent regarding any potential fulfillment when _he could easily have provided it_ — **_had it actually occurred!_** This is especially notable as Luke was so descriptive in documenting the fulfillment of _the second part of Paul's prophecy,_ devoting over a chapter to it!

Logic would rather infer that Luke would be as descriptive for the former as for the latter (**'_It seemed good to me also, having had perfect understanding of all things from the very first, to write unto thee in order, most excellent Theophilus,_'** – Luke 1:3)!

Moreover, if this prophecy of Paul did not occur, then what does that say about the so–called angelic being?

---

[29] Acts 27:23-24 23 For there stood by me this night the angel of God, whose I am, and whom I serve, 24 Saying, Fear not, Paul; thou must be brought before Caesar: and, lo, God hath given thee all them that sail with thee.

Wasn't there supposed to have been an angelic being that appeared to Paul 'on the road to Damascus?'[30] Doesn't this later event grant us license to question whether that initial *spiritual encounter* would have been from the Most-High-God?

Paul claimed to be an Apostle of Jesus, and this claim could only be corroborated and authenticated by his own private accounts from his own **secret** visions and revelations.

According to the Christian Bible, Paul proclaimed that he was appointed to be an Apostle by a spirit appearing to him in a vision, **identifying himself as the risen Jesus!**

However, *if Paul never even met the real Jesus in the flesh,* just how would he have been able to know it was the risen Jesus who was speaking to him?

> If I bear witness of myself, my witness is not true. [John 5:31]

Jesus is said to have spoken, *"If I bear witness of myself, my witness is not true."* **If Jesus is the greater,** the head as it were, then shouldn't that apply to the subservient Paul as well?

Claiming to have had visions and revelations are the singular **proof-claims** by which Paul proclaimed that he was personally chosen to be an Apostle by Jesus!

Further, **Paul's self-proclamations as the *greatest Apostle*,** by the few moments he claims to have spent with *his familiar spirit friend, whom he called Jesus* — *in private visions and revelations* — of course, those claims are supposed to **supersede** any and all teachings that occurred in the time that the handpicked Apostles spent with the real flesh and blood

---

[30] Acts 9:1-31; Acts 22:1-16; Acts 26:12-20. You may notice that each account is fundamentally different; though similar, they do not completely agree with each other!

Jesus! The New Testament records that each and every one of those other men were personal friends or relatives of Jesus!

To reiterate, the self–appointed — *UBER* Apostle Paul —
NEVER EVEN MET THE MAN, JESUS!

Thus, I have to ask, *"If Paul had not previously known Jesus personally, then how could he possibly have been able to recognize him by sight and by the sound of his voice?"*

Also, would it not be reasonable to think that, as a **new believer,** Paul should have wanted to immediately go to the only living, close sources of information about the life of Jesus, the original, well known handpicked Apostles themselves?

After all, Luke quotes Paul:

> [3] I am verily a man which am a Jew, born in Tarsus, a city in Cilicia, yet brought up in this city at the feet of Gamaliel, and taught according to the perfect manner of the law of the fathers, and was zealous toward God, as ye all are this day.
> [Acts 22:3]

Paul claimed to have been a disciple of Gamaliel, one of the leading rabbis of his day. He said that he "was brought up in this city at the feet of Gamaliel." **Yet, apparently, he was not willing to also sit at the feet of the Apostles of Jesus,** even soon after the point in time he claims as his *profound conversion to his new faith in Jesus!*

From Galatians 1:17, it is quite evident that from the very first moments after his vision, **Paul considered that he was**

consequently a full member among the remaining twelve originals, *a bona fide Apostle of Jesus Christ!*

Moreover, in that first moment *before he was changed* into a *'new believer in Jesus as the Messiah,' how could he have been already filled with the 'Holy Spirit'* to know and discern that his vision was legitimate and approved by Almighty God?

His own recorded words convict him in his arrogance!

"Neither went I up to Jerusalem to them which were apostles before me; ...*Then after three years...*"

> 17 Neither went I up to Jerusalem to them which were apostles before me; but I went into Arabia, and returned again unto Damascus.
> 18 Then after three years I went up to Jerusalem to see Peter, and abode with him fifteen days.
> 19 But other of the apostles saw I none, save James the Lord's brother.
> 20 Now the things which I write unto you, behold, before God, I lie not.
> 21 Afterwards I came into the regions of Syria and Cilicia;
> 22 And was unknown by face unto the churches of Judaea which were in Christ:
> 23 But they had heard only, That he which persecuted us in times past now preacheth the faith which once he destroyed.
> 24 And they glorified God in me. [Gal. 1:17-24]

[1] Then fourteen years after I went up again to Jerusalem with Barnabas, and took Titus with me also. [Galatians 2:1]

Clearly, Paul had no desire to 'sit at the feet of' and learn directly from the very people who actually knew Jesus personally. Those men were *handpicked by Jesus to be his particular emissaries,* to carry forth his message!

Paul expressed that he had *no interest* in learning directly from them, by 'sitting at their feet!' He had certainly been willing to sit at the feet of Gamaliel. **Why not the Apostles?**

Yet, from the first moments in his vision, *Paul included himself among the 'elite'* Apostles of Jesus. Surprisingly, he actually had no direct knowledge – **nor apparent interest** – in knowing about the teachings and even way of life of the man, Jesus!

Rather, by his own words **he went off on his own for three years, then an additional fourteen years, and created the new religion** which became known as '**Christianity,**' *based upon his own claims from his private, personal,* **demonic** *encounters with Ghosts and Familiar Spirits!*

Yes, you read me correctly! I said and I meant **demonic** – i.e. **no**t of Yehovah, **not** *sanctioned* by the Almighty! If I am correct, Paul had *familiar spirit friends* who guided him in his ministry! He never met the man, Jesus! **How would he have been able to *discern* that the visions were truly of Jesus?**

Demonic Ghosts and Familiar Spirits

Turn ye not unto the ghosts, nor unto familiar spirits; seek them not out, to be

defiled by them: I am Yehovah your God. [Leviticus 19:31]

And the soul that turneth unto the ghosts, and unto the familiar spirits, to go astray after them, I will even set My face against that soul, and will cut him off from among his people. [Leviticus 20:6]

A man also or a woman that divineth by a ghost or a familiar spirit, shall surely be put to death; they shall stone them with stones; their blood shall be upon them. [Leviticus 20:27]

I realize that **Paul said that his familiar spirit friend identified himself as Jesus.** I have to ask you, is it recorded anywhere else that *the risen Jesus* ever appeared to anyone else after the immediacy of the events around the time of his death?

Many chosen Apostles, personal friends or relatives of Jesus have books attributed to them in the New Testament. Except for the Revelation to John, do any of them suggest that they had a private, secret, spiritual encounter with the recognizable, *risen Jesus,* **after the immediate events** around his execution?

NO! *Only Saul of Tarsus,* **Paul – consultor of Ghosts and Familiar Spirits. He is the inventor, the definer of its doctrines, and the chief architect for what became known as the emergent, new and foreign religion – Christianity.**

Since Paul never knew Jesus personally, *he obviously never got the following 'memo'* (notification):

3 And as he sat upon the mount of Olives, the disciples came unto him privately, saying, Tell us, when shall these things be? and what shall be the sign of thy coming, and of the end of the world?
4 And Jesus answered and said unto them, Take heed that no man deceive you.
5 For many shall come in my name, saying, I am Christ; and shall deceive many.

23 Then if any man shall say unto you, Lo, here is Christ, or there; believe it not.
24 For there shall arise false Christs, and false prophets, and shall shew great signs and wonders; insomuch that, if it were possible, they shall deceive the very elect.
25 Behold, I have told you before.
26 Wherefore if they shall say unto you, Behold, he is in the desert; go not forth: behold, he is in the secret chambers; believe it not.
27 For as the lightning cometh out of the east, and shineth even unto the west; so shall also the coming of the Son of man be.
[Matthew 24:3-5, 23-27]

Shouldn't that admonition have applied to Paul as well?

Followers of Paul might emphasize that Paul never even met the real, flesh and blood Jesus, and, thus, he had not been made aware of these warnings by Jesus! Thus, quite obviously, that meant *Jesus's admonition didn't apply to him!*

That is, sort of, similar in our modern age when astronaut Alan Bean essentially said, regarding the **deadly Van Allen Radiation Belt,** starting about 1,000 miles from earth and extending 25,000 miles between earth and the Moon — ***that it didn't affect 'them' because 'they' didn't know about it!***[31]

I believe that the Matthew 24 warnings lend credence to my assertion that **'the being identifying himself as Jesus,'** that appeared to Paul, was actually a **demonic, *familiar spirit.***

Moreover, Matthew 24:3 starts off with a question regarding Jesus's return and the end of the world. I am of the opinion that Saul of Tarsus, aka Paul, **is part of the end-time deception!**

Apparently, **ignorant and gullible people refuse to question Paul,** who has liberated them, made them free, from following THE DIVINE LAW – **The Torah of Yehovah,** as well as the rest of the Hebrew-language based Jewish Scriptures!

In his writings, *Paul often spoke against the Torah* when he mentioned any of its statutes or commandments!

> [1] Stand fast therefore in the liberty wherewith Christ hath made us free, and be not entangled again with the yoke of bondage.
> [2] Behold, I Paul say unto you, that if ye be circumcised, Christ shall profit you nothing.
> [3] For I testify again to every man that is circumcised, that he is a debtor to do the whole law.
> [4] Christ is become of no effect unto you, whosoever of you are justified by the law; ye are fallen from grace.

---

[31] Van Allen Belts NASA Hoax Alan Bean, YouTube video accessed 15 Mar 2023, https://www.youtube.com/watch?v=F_6RB65gnIE.

⁵ For we through the Spirit wait for the hope of righteousness by faith.

⁶ For in Jesus Christ neither circumcision availeth any thing, nor uncircumcision; but faith which worketh by love. [Galatians 5:1-6]

Also, Reading 'Jesus' Into The Jewish Text

Just as many 'Pauline Christians' mentally **insert the name "Jesus"** when they see attributions to **"God"** when reading the Jewish Scriptures, perhaps when reading Paul and we read "Jesus Christ" as in Galatians 5:6, 'For in Jesus Christ ..." we should also have a license to insert something like, **'For in Paul's demonic familiar spirit** *friend* **he called Jesus Christ,'** neither circumcision availeth any thing, nor uncircumcision; but faith which worketh by love.'

I want to emphasize that the real Jesus said, **'For many shall come in my name, saying, I am Christ; and shall deceive many.'** (Matthew 24:5). *His true followers understood this.*

Yet, the self-appointed Apostle Paul based *all* **of his own knowledge and authority on his own** *demonic visions!*

The Galatians 5:3 verse actually self-convicts Paul, in his statement, **"For I testify again to every man that is circumcised, that he is a debtor to do the whole law."**

It should be known that **there is no place in the entire Jewish Scriptures that makes that declaration!** Circumcision was the sign of the covenant for males.³² Isaac was the first child conceived by Abraham and Sarah after Abraham was

---

³² Elon Gilad, 'Circumcision, a Symbol of the Jews' Covenant with God,' last modified 26 Aug 2015, https://www.haaretz.com/jewish/2015-08-26/ty-article/circumcision-a-symbol-of-the-jews-covenant-with-god/0000017f-e37d-d9aa-afff-fb7d02fb0000.

circumcised at age ninety-nine! Per that covenant, Isaac would have been circumcised at eight days old.

Unfortunately, Paul boldly stated, '... to every man that is circumcised, that he is a debtor to do the whole law' — *just as if it was a well known dictum in Judaism, and supported by the authority of the Jewish Scripture!*

This is a manner typical of Paul — it is truly a subterfuge. He played *'fast and loose with Holy Scriptures,'* claiming to honestly quote from them. This appears to be an attempt to authenticate his cavalier statements, especially when there were absolutely no bona fide Scriptural references to back up his claims.

Gullible believers do not question Paul! It appears that non-Jewish people get excited over the idea of inheriting all of the positive promises to the Jewish people but that they are allowed to continue living outside of the Torah as if it is not just done away with but more so that they may consider it *of the devil!*[33]

So, do I also have the right to insert something like *'Paul's demonic familiar spirit friend who he said identified himself as Jesus'* anytime I see Paul mention Jesus?

If I did this, Galatians 5:1-6 might be rendered thusly:

> [1] Stand fast therefore in the liberty wherewith *'my demonic familiar spirit friend calling himself [Christ]'* hath made us free, and be not entangled again with the yoke of bondage.
> [2] Behold, I Paul say unto you, that if ye be circumcised, *'my demonic familiar spirit friend calling himself [Christ]'* shall profit you nothing.

---

[33] Glenn Paauw, 'The Satan and The Law That Enslaves (Powers & Principalities, Pt. 3),' INSTITUTE FOR BIBLE READING, last modified 9 Jul 2020, https://instituteforbiblereading.org/the-satan-and-the-law-that-enslaves/.

3 For I testify again to every man that is circumcised, that he is a debtor to do the whole law.

4 *'My demonic familiar spirit friend calling himself [Christ]'* is become of no effect unto you, whosoever of you are justified by the law; ye are fallen from grace.

5 For we through the *[demonic]* Spirit wait for the hope of righteousness by faith.

6 For in *'my demonic familiar spirit friend calling himself [Jesus Christ]'* neither circumcision availeth any thing, nor uncircumcision; but faith which worketh by love. [Galatians 5:1-6 **with my *bold embellishments*]**

I want to reiterate that Jesus gave a warning to his followers: *'...Take heed that no man deceive you. For many shall come in my name, saying, I am Christ, and shall deceive many.'* [Matthew 24:4b-5].

Since Paul clearly was deceived, he also has deceived many! Are you one of those who *enjoy this deception*?

From Jesus's own warning, isn't it easily seen that the beings in the private visions of the self-appointed Apostle Paul fall into the category of ***demons, ghosts and familiar spirits?***

Weren't the beings in Paul's spiritual visions essentially **saying, 'I am Christ?' Jesus made it abundantly clear that he would *not* be appearing, essentially in private, secret visions,** declaring that anyone who had such **could not be trusted** as legitimately following Jesus and more so, of the Almighty-God, Yehovah Himself!

Thus, **according to Jesus's recorded words in Matthew 24, the spirits in Paul's visions should actually be considered to be *false, lying, demonic and familiar spirits*!**

Essentially, by Jesus's own words, **Paul was clearly deceived!**

Those who submit to Paul's authority and the body of his teachings have likewise participated in the contaminated stream of doctrines based upon Paul's spiritual deception!

Moreover, where are the independent testimonials of the people who were supposed to have been with Saul of Tarsus on the road to Damascus? If there were any written accounts, none of the early writers seemed to think they were important enough to help validate Paul's claims. Also, because Luke claimed that he had essentially consulted all available witnesses, why would he have been silent about this as well?

Essentially, there are no independent, corroborating and surviving testimonies recorded in the Christian New Testament that can validate Paul and his *demonic visions!*

Further, even though Paul never met the real flesh and blood Jesus, he was still subject to the admonition of Jesus, "For many shall come in my name, saying, I am Christ, and shall deceive many." [Matthew 24:4-5]

Yet, to much of Christianity, aka Paul's followers, everything he wrote is absolutely God-breathed Scripture! Thus, in essence and to them, to question Paul is tantamount to questioning the Almighty, and is essentially blasphemy!

Isn't accepting Paul as a true Apostle *a simple rejection* of the warning of Jesus, "...For many shall come in my name, saying, I am Christ."?

... by the mouth of two or three witnesses ... If by the mouth of two or three witnesses a matter is resolved in the Torah of יְהֹוָה (Yehovah [YHVH]), **how is it that Paul's claims are not allowed to be verified by anyone except himself?**

6 At the mouth of two witnesses, or three witnesses, shall he that is to die be put to death; at the mouth of one witness he shall not be put to death. [Deuteronomy 17:6]

15 One witness shall not rise up against a man for any iniquity, or for any sin, in any sin that he sinneth; at the mouth of two witnesses, or at the mouth of three witnesses, shall a matter be established.
16 If an unrighteous witness rise up against any man to bear perverted witness against him;
17 then both the men, between whom the controversy is, shall stand before Yehovah, before the priests and the judges that shall be in those days.
18 And the judges shall inquire diligently; and, behold, if the witness be a false witness, and hath testified falsely against his brother;
19 then shall ye do unto him, as he had purposed to do unto his brother; so shalt thou put away the evil from the midst of thee.
20 And those that remain shall hear, and fear, and shall henceforth commit no more any such evil in the midst of thee.
21 And thine eye shall not pity: life for life, eye for eye, tooth for tooth, hand for hand, foot for foot. [Deuteronomy 19:15-21]

Ironically, Paul's claims to Apostleship are based upon his own unchallenged accounts! **Each of his encounters** with his **demonic _familiar spirit friend,_** whom he said identified as Jesus, **_all occurred within his own private, secret visions._**

Those considered to be legitimate Apostles walked personally with the real, flesh and blood Jesus. They were all well aware of Jesus's admonition regarding anyone, thereafter, coming **in _his name,_ deceiving many — _and, of such, was Paul_!**

Simply stated, **the self-appointed Apostle Paul was _NOT_ a legitimate Apostle of Jesus,** nor should he be treated as if he were a man of the Most-High-God.

He was a monumental deceiver and clearly a false prophet!

I believe I would be remiss if I failed to bring up the idea of the nature of a prophet other than just understanding it in the terms of prophesying, foretelling future events. The following quote may help to provide a better understanding of a prophet from a Jewish frame of reference:

What is a Prophet?

Many people today think of a prophet as any person who sees the future. While the gift of prophecy certainly includes the ability to see the future, a prophet is far more than just a person with that ability.

A prophet is basically a spokesman for G-d, a person chosen by G-d to speak to people on G-d's behalf and convey a message or teaching. Prophets were role models of holiness, scholarship and closeness to G-d. They set the standards for the entire community.

The Hebrew word for a prophet, navi (Nun-Beit-Yod-Alef, נביא) is said to be related to the term niv sefatayim (נִיב שְׂפָתָיִם, Isaiah 57:19) meaning "fruit of the lips," which emphasizes the prophet's role as a speaker.[34]

The above referenced Isaiah passage is included for information:

בּוֹרֵא נִיב שְׂפָתָיִם שָׁלוֹם ׀ שָׁלוֹם
לָרָחוֹק וְלַקָּרוֹב אָמַר יְהוָה וּרְפָאתִיו:

Peace, peace, to him that is far off and to him that is near, saith Yehovah that createth the fruit of the lips; and I will heal him. [Isaiah 57:19]

Thus, it is important to know that a prophet is not just someone who forecasts the future, **but can also be someone teaching what Scripture can be understood to mean.**

I think it is very important for us to grasp this concept, as it could also apply to any one of us.

Thus, we must be very careful that we do not misrepresent the written words of the revelation of Yehovah [God] as found in the Hebrew-language based Jewish Scriptures!

---

[34] Tracy R. Rich, 'Judaism 101, Prophets and Prophecy, What is a Prophet?,' accessed 21 Mar 2023, https://www.jewfaq.org/prophets.

Not only was Saul of Tarsus — *the self-appointed Apostle Paul* — <u>a</u> <u>false</u> <u>prophet</u> in the classical sense that he gave at least one prophecy which failed to come to pass, he also misrepresented the written Torah in his many cavalier declarations and proclamations!

In much of his writings, the false prophet — the false apostle Paul, misquoted, took out of context and otherwise misrepresented the very words of the Almighty God.

Beware of false prophets, which come to you in sheep's clothing, but inwardly they are ravening wolves. [Matt. 7:15]

4 And Jesus answered and said unto them, Take heed that no man deceive you.
5 For many shall come in my name, saying, I am Christ; and shall deceive many.

23 Then if any man shall say unto you, Lo, here is Christ, or there; believe it not.
24 For there shall arise false Christs, and false prophets, and shall shew great signs and wonders; insomuch that, if it were possible, they shall deceive the very elect.
[Matthew 24:4-5, 23-24]

THE PLAIN MEANING

35

Taking Plain Meaning — OUT of CONTEXT!

"By understanding how to identify genuine U.S. Currency, we can more easily detect counterfeit bills," explained Special Agent James Ingram.[36]

The U.S. Secret Service trains its agents to be able to detect counterfeit bills by ***exposing them to genuine U.S. Currency!***

Obviously, there needs to be a ***legitimate base*** as a standard.

In the realm of religion, I posit that the ***Leningrad Codex***[37] is the ***genuine*** baseline for the Hebrew–Language based Jewish

---

[35] Image assembled from author's photograph; converted to grayscale and image posterization applied.
[36] Office of the Special Prosecutor - Republic of Palau, 'OSP Hosts U.S. Secret Service Counterfeit Currency Training,' accessed 28 Sep 2022, https://www.palauosp.org/2020/02/20/osp-hosts-ussecretservice-counterfeit-currencytraining/.
[37] Curt Leviant, 'Jewish Holy Scriptures: The Leningrad Codex,' Jewish Virtual Library, accessed 19 May 2022, https://www.jewishvirtuallibrary.org/the-leningrad-codex.

Scriptures! I am particularly fond of The Ten Commandments, especially those found in Exodus 20.[38] My intention is to read them at the beginning of my regular, daily, Scripture reading!

The following quote is an English translation of the ninth commandment, found in Exodus 20:

[11] **Thou shalt not bear false witness against thy neighbor.** [Exodus 20:11]

This verse is jam–packed with meaning. The two Hebrew words often translated as *false witness,* עֵד שָׁקֶר, (pronounced, Aid Sha-qair) at the end of the verse, are quite meaningful: עֵד (=witness, testimony)[39] and שָׁקֶר (=lie, falsehood, deception (by words))[40] should help in understanding this 'commandment.'

The plain and simple meaning of this verse is about *not* bearing a false/lying witness/testimony against one's neighbor. Typically, a court of law is where this sort of thing is applicable.

It should be obvious that *bearing a false witness before your neighbor* __is__ __an__ __egregious__ __sin.__ It was deemed important enough to be included among the Ten Commandments, written on tablets of stone by the Almighty God Himself!

A Modern-Day Example

In the United States, on September 26, 2019, California Congressman Adam Schiff presented before Congress and the American people, a *made–up* verbal rendition of a transcript from a telephone conversation between President Trump and

---

38 Robert M. Pill, 'The Real God Code: The Ten Commandments In The Leningrad Codex,' (Robert M. Pill, 2021), 'Why I Promote Exodus 20 Over Deuteronomy 5,' pp 43-44.
39 Ernest Klein, 'A Comprehensive Etymological Dictionary of the Hebrew Language for Readers of English' (Carta, Jerusalem), Copyright © 1987 by The Beatrice & Arthur Minden Foundation & The University of Haifa. Page 464, middle column, top.
40 ibid. Page 680, Left Column, Lower.

the President of Ukraine. That rendition made President Trump look like a corrupt, mean-spirited and nasty criminal, which could easily be construed as the ***intent*** by representative Schiff!

It certainly appears that those people who fell into the camp of **already** *hating* President Trump saw Adam Schiff as expressing unmitigated truth — that he was representing, as he claimed, ***the exact essence of the words of the President***.

In an attempt to apparently protect himself, and, no doubt, using guarded language from his training as a lawyer, Adam Schiff claimed that his rendition was the essence of the conversation.

It is my opinion that Adam Schiff was well aware that many in his audience would only hear what they thought was the reading of the actual transcript of the conversation.

Also, I believe that he was attempting to obscure the fact that he was presenting a totally false narrative having little or nothing to do with the actual conversation, let alone the essence of that conversation!

However, anyone who actually attempted to read the transcript of the phone conversation could have easily determined that ***Adam Schiff had borne a false witness to the American people of his blatant made–up, lying misrepresentation of a conversation of the sitting President.***[41]

---

[41] "President Trump on Friday called on Rep. Adam Schiff to resign, accusing the Democratic chairman of the House Intelligence Committee of lying by reading to Congress a phony version of his call with the Ukrainian president."

"Rep. Adam Schiff fraudulently read to Congress, with millions of people watching, a version of my conversation with the President of Ukraine that doesn't exist," Trump wrote in a series of tweets."

"He was supposedly reading the exact transcribed version of the call, but he completely changed the words to make it sound horrible, and me sound guilty. HE WAS DESPERATE AND HE GOT CAUGHT."

Falsely Representing
The Testimony Of The Original Source

Since I am wanting to express how the **ninth commandment** may apply to misrepresenting the context and plain meaning of the authoritative, Hebrew-language based Jewish Scriptural source, I would apply to it the nuanced definition of *'falsely representing the testimony of the original source!'*

In my opinion, quoting from a known, authoritative source, and taking it out of its plain and natural context, is a clear example of <u>breaking</u> <u>the</u> <u>ninth</u> <u>commandment</u>!

A LIE, Believed By Many, Does NOT Make It TRUE!

Left unchecked, misquotes and quotations taken out of their plain and natural context become truth to those who do not bother to verify them. *However, a lie believed by many does not make it true — even to a few!*

In the process of referencing a source, most people appear to give the impression that they are quoting a passage, in context, and providing the commonly understood interpretation. In so doing, they represent themselves as arbiters of truth; and most people who believe them do not even consider that they may possibly be lying!

Within the Christian Scriptures this appears to be a common practice by one particular author. *Suffice it to say that it is an especially flagrant abuse of trust.*

"Adam Schiff therefore lied to Congress and attempted to defraud the American Public. He has been doing this for two years. I am calling for him to immediately resign from Congress based on this fraud!" Trump continued.

Yaron Steinbuch, 'Trump calls on Adam Schiff to resign for allegedly lying to Congress,' New York Post, September 27, 2019, 8:32 a.m., updated, https://nypost.com/2019/09/27/trump-calls-on-adam-schiff-to-resign-for-allegedly-lying-to-congress/.

Deceiving Gentiles By Attributing Promises In Jewish Scripture As Applying To Them!

Ironically, that deceptive practice has been most often perpetrated by the one promoting himself to be the preeminent Apostle of Jesus![42] That author is none other than the aforementioned Saul of Tarsus, well known in Christendom as 'The Apostle Paul.' It is he who is the chief definer of doctrine!

Starting from **indirectly referencing** the books of **Hosea** and **Isaiah** as his authority in the book of **Romans,** there is a blatant abuse of trust — of misquoting the Holy Scriptures — by forcing an interpretation away from a natural context directed to the Israelite people (Jews) and applying it to non-Jews (Gentiles)!

I will first quote from the first part of this Romans 9 example:

> 22 What if God, willing to shew his wrath, and to make his power known, endured with much longsuffering the vessels of wrath fitted to destruction:
> 23 And that he might make known the riches of his glory on the vessels of mercy, which he had afore prepared unto glory,
> 24 Even us, whom he hath called, not of the Jews only, but also of the Gentiles?
> 25 As he saith also in Osee, I will call them my people, which were not my people; and her beloved, which was not beloved.
> 26 And it shall come to pass, that in the place where it was said unto them, Ye are

---

[42] Christian New Testament, book of 2 Corinthians, Chapter 11:5 (KJV): **"For I suppose I was not a whit behind the very chiefest apostles."** and in the book of Colossians, Chapter 1:24 (KJV) **"Who now rejoice in my sufferings for you, and fill up that which is behind of the afflictions of Christ in my flesh for his body's sake, which is the church:"**

not my people; there shall they be called
the children of the living God.
[Romans 9:22-26]

That Romans passage certainly makes it appear that the
quoted passage from Hosea **_proves_** that Paul's audience will
receive the promises found therein!

However, **I will actually show the context of who the Hosea
passage is directed,** found in Hosea 2:1-2, followed by Hosea
2:25, the verse Paul attributes to Gentiles:

> **¹ Yet the number of the children of
> Israel shall be as the sand of the sea,
> which cannot be measured nor
> numbered; and it shall come to pass
> that, instead of that which was said
> unto them: 'Ye are not My people', it
> shall be said unto them: 'Ye are the
> children of the living God.'
> ² And the children of Judah and the
> children of Israel shall be gathered
> together, and they shall appoint
> themselves one head, and shall go up
> out of the land; for great shall be the
> day of Jezreel.**

> **²⁵ And I will sow her unto Me in the land;
> and I will have compassion upon her
> that had not obtained compassion; and
> I will say to them that were not My
> people: 'Thou art My people'; and they
> shall say: 'Thou art my God.'**
> [Hosea 2:1-2, 25]

Thus, from the context of Hosea 2, it is quite clear that Hosea's prophecy is directed only to the Israelite, Jewish people! There is absolutely no indication from the prophecy that it should apply to any future non-Israelite or mixed people, even though Paul eloquently expresses it to be so in his book of Romans!

I believe that this is truly a _clever deception,_ and that it is an intentional breach of the ninth commandment!

The Romans 9 passage continues, attempting to quote Isaiah:

> 27 Esaias also crieth concerning Israel, Though the number of the children of Israel be as the sand of the sea, a remnant shall be saved:
> 28 For he will finish the work, and cut it short in righteousness: because a short work will the Lord make upon the earth. [Romans 9:27-28]

... and, within its context, the referenced passage from Isaiah:

> **20 And it shall come to pass in that day, that the remnant of Israel, and they that are escaped of the house of Jacob, shall no more again stay upon him that smote them; but shall stay upon Yehovah, the Holy One of Israel, in truth.**
> **21 A remnant shall return, even the remnant of Jacob, unto God the Mighty.**
> **22 For though thy people, O Israel, be as the sand of the sea, only a remnant of**

them shall return; an extermination is determined, overflowing with righteousness.
23 For an extermination wholly determined shall the Lord GOD of Hosts [Adonai Yehovi Tze-va'ot] make in the midst of all the earth.
24 Therefore thus saith the Lord GOD of Hosts [Adonai Yehovi Tze-va'ot]: O My people that dwellest in Zion, be not afraid of Asshur, though he smite thee with the rod, and lift up his staff against thee, after the manner of Egypt.
[Isaiah 10:20-24]

I believe the Isaiah 10 passage is the intended reference by Paul for Romans 9:27-28. **Quite obviously, <u>quoting</u> <u>it</u> <u>has</u> <u>little,</u> <u>if</u> <u>anything,</u> <u>to</u> <u>do</u> <u>with</u> <u>the</u> <u>context</u> <u>of</u> <u>its</u> <u>source</u>!**

Again, referencing the prophet Isaiah, **Romans 9 continues:**

29 And as Esaias said before, Except the Lord of Sabaoth had left us a seed, we had been as Sodoma, and been made like unto Gomorrha.
30 What shall we say then? That the Gentiles, which followed not after righteousness, have attained to righteousness, even the righteousness which is of faith.
31 But Israel, which followed after the law of righteousness, hath not attained to the law of righteousness.
32 Wherefore? Because they sought it not by faith, but as it were by the works of the law. For they stumbled at that stumblingstone;

³³ As it is written, Behold, I lay in Sion a stumblingstone and rock of offence: and whosoever believeth on him shall not be ashamed. [Romans 9:27-33]

So, where did Isaiah express those thoughts?

Well, *it depends on which source of the 'Jewish Scriptures' you choose to use!* In the '**English Septuagint**,'⁴³ the passage is rendered similarly to Romans 9:33 (KJV), above:

¹⁶ Therefore thus saith the Lord, even the Lord, Behold, I lay for the foundations of Sion a costly stone, a choice, a corner-stone, a precious stone, for its foundations; and he that believes on him shall by no means be ashamed. [Isaiah 28:16 – English Septuagint⁴⁴]

On the other hand, if you use an *authoritative Jewish source* based upon the Leningrad Codex, such as that found in *The Pill Tanakh,* the same verse is translated a bit differently:

¹⁶ **Therefore thus saith the Lord GOD [Adonai Yehovi]: Behold, I lay in Zion for a foundation a stone, a tried stone, a costly corner-stone of sure foundation; he that believeth shall not make haste.** [Isaiah 28:16]

The Isaiah 28 passage, below, should help show Paul's great deception in misquoting it and taking it out of its natural context:

---

⁴³ Lancelot Charles Lee Brenton, 'English Translation of the Septuagint,' Samuel Bagster & Sons, Ltd., London, 1851.
⁴⁴ ibid.

9 Whom shall one teach knowledge? And whom shall one make to understand the message? Them that are weaned from the milk, them that are drawn from the breasts?

10 For it is precept by precept, precept by precept, line by line, line by line; here a little, there a little.

11 For with stammering lips and with a strange tongue shall it be spoken to this people;

12 To whom it was said: 'This is the rest, give ye rest to the weary; and this is the refreshing'; yet they would not hear.

13 And so the word of Yehovah is unto them precept by precept, precept by precept, line by line, line by line; here a little, there a little; that they may go, and fall backward, and be broken, and snared, and taken.

14 Wherefore hear the word of Yehovah, ye scoffers, the ballad-mongers of this people which is in Yerushalam:

15 Because ye have said: 'We have made a covenant with death, and with the nether-world are we at agreement; when the scouring scourge shall pass through, it shall not come unto us; for we have made lies our refuge, and in falsehood have we hid ourselves';

16 **Therefore thus saith the Lord GOD [Adonai Yehovi]: Behold, I lay in Zion for a foundation a stone, a tried stone, a costly corner-stone of sure foundation; he that believeth shall not make haste.**

17 And I will make justice the line, and righteousness the plummet; and the hail shall sweep away the refuge of lies, and the waters shall overflow the hiding-place. [Isaiah 28:9-17]

Why is there such a discrepancy between Paul's quotes and the context of their referenced sources in Jewish Scripture?

Also, **why** are the Septuagint and the New Testament (even that in the King James Version) **aligned** in their interpretation **but sufficiently different** than the contexts of their referenced sources from the ancient Hebrew of the Leningrad Codex?

Perhaps the reason can be understood by reexamining just what the Greek Septuagint is and why it should be important to know its real history as well as some Scriptural criticism.

Simply stated, two-thirds (2/3) of the three hundred or so 'Old Testament' quotes in the Christian New Testament are from the Greek Septuagint instead of the actual Hebrew-language based Jewish Scriptures! I discussed this back in my first chapter, 'Influence.' I also quoted **David Daniels** in his book, **'Did Jesus Use The Septuagint?'** Please refer back to my first chapter to see just a snippet of his great analysis! **I also encourage you to read his book and watch his video series on that subject.**

The Curse of the Law
The Christian Doctrine of "The Curse Of The Law?"

In the Christian Scriptures, the term **'the Law'** appears to have become synonymous with the Hebrew term **'the Torah.'**

I find it rather ironic that **the term 'Law' has such a negative connotation within Christian thinking, theology, practice and expression!**

The **source for this idea** appears to be found in the iconic statement of the Apostle Paul from his book of Galatians.

> [13] Christ hath redeemed us from the curse
> of the law, being made a curse for us: for

it is written, Cursed is every one that hangeth on a tree:

14 That the blessing of Abraham might come on the Gentiles through Jesus Christ; that we might receive the promise of the Spirit through faith. [Galatians 3:13-14]

I am hoping that you will grasp the real implications and the intent of its author, Paul. The interpretation of the phrase, *'Cursed is everyone who is hanged on a tree'* – carries much of the weight of Christian doctrine, regarding law, 'on its back!'

To me, this Galatians passage is not merely in error but also deceptive on many levels!

First and foremost, **the quote is *just part of a verse,*** a snippet, and it does not provide the context of the referenced verse!

At the end of verse 13, it says, "For it is written, Cursed is everyone who is hanged on a tree."

It is noteworthy, that phrase within its New Testament context, has absolutely no correlating passage, in context, in the entire Hebrew–language based Jewish Scriptures (aka, what most Christians refer to as the **Old Testament**)!

The statement *'cursed is everyone who is hanged on a tree'* is only found in Paul's book of Galatians. *Again, it is not found to be in context in its presumptive source, the Hebrew–language based Jewish Scriptures!*

To those who are able to question this phrase in Galatians:

If the self–appointed Apostle Paul, who claimed to have been **a Hebrew of the Hebrews** — who was even from that statement, presumably, fully informed of the Hebrew–language based Jewish Scriptures — actually wrote or dictated this passage in

Galatians, he could not have been quite so familiar with those Jewish Scriptures as the term 'Hebrew of the Hebrews' would suggest; and **he was, therefore, an abject liar.**

Otherwise, he was aware that he was taking Holy Scripture out of its natural context, and **thus, he was a purposeful deceiver.**

Either of those cases *should trouble* those who hold Paul in such high esteem as to believe he was the preeminent Apostle, the chief architect of doctrine, the chief spokesperson of Jesus, and that his writings are tantamount to "The Word of God!"

The 'Curse' In The Jewish Scriptures: Only When A Body Remains Hung After The Sun Sets!

As a matter of fact, the Hebrew–language based Jewish Scriptures only speak of a *curse* regarding someone hung on a tree **when that person's body *remains hung after the setting of the sun!***

The curse has absolutely no correlation with the act of hanging itself, as the Galatians passage suggests, but only to the *corpse remaining hung after the setting of the sun.*

This is quite evident by looking at the three Hebrew-language based Jewish Scripture passages speaking about this subject (Deuteronomy 21:22-23; Joshua 8:29; 10:26-27):

> **22 And if a man have committed a sin worthy of death, and he be put to death, and thou hang him on a tree;**
> **23 his body shall not remain all night upon the tree, but thou shalt surely bury him the same day; for he that is hanged is a reproach unto God; that thou defile not thy land which Yehovah**

thy God giveth thee for an inheritance.
[Deuteronomy 21:22-23]

29 And the king of Ai he hanged on a tree until the eventide; and at the going down of the sun Joshua commanded, and they took his carcass down from the tree, and cast it at the entrance of the gate of the city, and raised thereon a great heap of stones, unto this day.
[Joshua 8:29]

26 And afterward Joshua smote them, and put them to death, and hanged them on five trees; and they were hanging upon the trees until the evening.
27 And it came to pass at the time of the going down of the sun, that Joshua commanded, and they took them down off the trees, and cast them into the cave wherein they had hidden themselves, and laid great stones on the mouth of the cave, unto this very day. [Joshua 10:26-27]

Only by taking Deuteronomy 21:23 *out of the plain meaning in its natural context* can it be interpreted to say that the act of hanging itself is a curse. **By just quoting part of the verse** from the source in the Hebrew–language based Jewish Scriptures, the Galatians passage clearly *takes the original out of context and obfuscates its meaning.*

Again, in its natural context, Deuteronomy 21:23 clearly states that _a **corpse** remaining **hung** after **sunset** is **that which causes** 'the **curse**.'_

Moreover, the above referenced passages in Joshua 8 and 10 show the carrying out of the Scriptural command in taking hung bodies down before sunset. By knowing that there is a **curse** for leaving bodies hung on a tree after the setting of the sun, **Joshua fully understood the Scriptural command, and was obedient in carrying it out.**

Jesus's Body Did Not Remain Hung On The Cross After Sunset!

Quite telling is that, according to the Christian Bible, _**there is absolutely no indication that the body of Jesus remained hung on the cross (tree) after the setting of the sun.**_[45]

---

[45] Jesus Is Buried (Passages From King James Version)
Matthew 27:57-61
[57] When the even was come, there came a rich man of Arimathaea, named Joseph, who also himself was Jesus' disciple:
[58] He went to Pilate, and begged the body of Jesus. Then Pilate commanded the body to be delivered.
[59] And when Joseph had taken the body, he wrapped it in a clean linen cloth,
[60] And laid it in his own new tomb, which he had hewn out in the rock: and he rolled a great stone to the door of the sepulchre, and departed.
[61] And there was Mary Magdalene, and the other Mary, sitting over against the sepulchre.

Mark 15:42-47
[42] And now when the even was come, because it was the preparation, that is, the day before the sabbath,
[43] Joseph of Arimathaea, an honourable counsellor, which also waited for the kingdom of God, came, and went in boldly unto Pilate, and craved the body of Jesus.
[44] And Pilate marvelled if he were already dead: and calling unto him the centurion, he asked him whether he had been any while dead.
[45] And when he knew it of the centurion, he gave the body to Joseph.
[46] And he bought fine linen, and took him down, and wrapped him in the linen, and laid him in a sepulchre which was hewn out of a rock, and rolled a stone unto the door of the sepulchre.
[47] And Mary Magdalene and Mary the mother of Joses beheld where he was laid.

Luke 23:50-56
[50] And, behold, there was a man named Joseph, a counsellor; and he was a good man, and a just:
[51] (The same had not consented to the counsel and deed of them;) he was of Arimathaea, a city of the Jews: who also himself waited for the kingdom of God.

It should easily be seen that **any <u>idea</u> of <u>Jesus</u> being a *curse*** cannot be based upon the referenced source, because his body did not remain hung after the setting of the sun! The context of the attributed Scriptural source clearly shows that <u>a</u> <u>body</u> <u>remaining</u> <u>hung</u> <u>on</u> <u>a</u> <u>tree</u> **after sunset** <u>is</u> <u>what</u> <u>causes</u> <u>a</u> **curse**.

Therefore, Paul's **'Christian' doctrine** relating to *'Christ redeemed us from the curse of the law by becoming a curse for us'* <u>is</u> <u>without</u> <u>merit</u>, having no credible foundation according to the actual 'Word of God' found in the written Torah!

---

52   This man went unto Pilate, and begged the body of Jesus.
53   And he took it down, and wrapped it in linen, and laid it in a sepulchre that was hewn in stone, wherein never man before was laid.
54   And that day was the preparation, and the sabbath drew on.
55   And the women also, which came with him from Galilee, followed after, and beheld the sepulchre, and how his body was laid.
56   And they returned, and prepared spices and ointments; and rested the sabbath day according to the commandment.

John 19:31-42
31 The Jews therefore, because it was the preparation, that the bodies should not remain upon the cross on the sabbath day, (for that sabbath day was an high day,) besought Pilate that their legs might be broken, and that they might be taken away.
32 Then came the soldiers, and brake the legs of the first, and of the other which was crucified with him.
33 But when they came to Jesus, and saw that he was dead already, they brake not his legs:
34 But one of the soldiers with a spear pierced his side, and forthwith came there out blood and water.
35 And he that saw it bare record, and his record is true: and he knoweth that he saith true, that ye might believe.
36 For these things were done, that the scripture should be fulfilled, A bone of him shall not be broken.
37 And again another scripture saith, They shall look on him whom they pierced.
38 And after this Joseph of Arimathaea, being a disciple of Jesus, but secretly for fear of the Jews, besought Pilate that he might take away the body of Jesus: and Pilate gave him leave. He came therefore, and took the body of Jesus.
39 And there came also Nicodemus, which at the first came to Jesus by night, and brought a mixture of myrrh and aloes, about an hundred pound weight.
40 Then took they the body of Jesus, and wound it in linen clothes with the spices, as the manner of the Jews is to bury.
41 Now in the place where he was crucified there was a garden; and in the garden a new sepulchre, wherein was never man yet laid.
42 There laid they Jesus therefore because of the Jews' preparation day; for the sepulchre was nigh at hand.

It is only through **Paul's assertion** that 'Christ became a curse for us' that the idea described in Galatians 3:14 gave his followers the ability **to receive promises made to Israel!**

> ¹⁴ That the blessing of Abraham might come on the Gentiles through Jesus Christ; that we might receive the promise of the Spirit through faith. [Galatians 3:14]

Paul's rendering is absolutely not just an incorrect interpretation **but also a great deception.** Again, in Galatians 3:14, **Paul attributes to Gentiles the inclusion into Israel, by faith,** based upon *his spurious interpretation* in the previous verse.

Paul was exceptionally subtle — deceiving many! I believe that a lying, Demonic Familiar Spirit was behind his inspirational deception!

Paul *arrogantly* took Jewish Scripture out of its natural context to construe an unnatural idea, especially to an audience that is not in the habit of testing his claims!

Yet, it is Paul's declaration which provides the doctrinal foundation for this concept of a curse of the Law in Christianity!

I believe that it is truly unfortunate for those people who absolutely believe that the Christian New Testament writings are entirely God–Breathed, and, more importantly, that since Paul said it, that obviously means it is unquestionably true; since, to them, his words contain no errors whatsoever, and, in fact, are equivalent to the very words of God!

I am of the opinion that many Christians are **complicit in joining Paul in *his demonic* deception!**

Taking Plain Meaning — OUT of CONTEXT!

I realize that I have only just touched on some of the misquotations of 'The Apostle Paul.' Nonetheless, I believe even that is enough to convict him of outrageous conduct in lying to a truly **gullible audience.** Taking Holy Scripture out of its natural context and misappropriating it **is an egregious sin!**

Likewise, making bold statements without any corroborating attributions is also a means of deception Paul has committed to his unquestioning audience.

Not only is Saul of Tarsus a false prophet, but he is also guilty of breaking the ninth commandment:

¹¹ **Thou shalt not bear false witness against thy neighbor.**
[Exodus 20:11]

The Israel of God?

46

Have Christians — Supplanted, i.e., Replaced Natural Israel?

Are Christians Now 'The Israel of God?'

To the abject exclusion of <u>natural</u> Israel, and without any sense of an obligation to follow the Torah, many Christians consider that they <u>alone</u> are now "<u>The</u> Israel <u>of</u> God!"[47]

Put another way, "By embracing the ethos of beliefs promulgated by the false prophet, the self-appointed Apostle Paul, many Christians consider that they have actually supplanted natural-born Israelites who were originally **sworn** to

---

[46] Rare Mangalitza pig - Essex - news.bbc.co.uk, "Rare Mangalitza pig being bred at Tropical Wings Zoo," last modified 14 April 2010,
http://news.bbc.co.uk/local/essex/hi/people_and_places/nature/newsid_8620000/8620329.stm.
Photo _47644821_mangalitza_pig_766.jpg converted to grayscale and image posterization applied.
[47] Michael Marlowe, "The Israel of God (Galatians 6:16)," Bible Researcher > Interpretation >Galatians 6:16, last modified Dec. 2004, https://www.bible-researcher.com/gal6-16.html.

be chosen to be the Children of Yehovah **forever!**" — **Some even express a belief that they are now, in fact, _Jewish_!**

Where might they have gotten such a _'nutty, grandiose'_ idea? ... **_Of course, from their own de facto (by-proxy) Messiah, their self-appointed, UBER–Apostle – Paul!_**

The Christian Bible (New Testament) is replete with many examples of this subterfuge.[48] It is exceptionally poignant in the books of **Galatians** (Chapter 6) and **Acts** (Chapter 15)!

> [12] As many as desire to make a fair shew in the flesh, they constrain you to be circumcised; only lest they should suffer persecution for the cross of Christ.
> [13] For neither they themselves who are circumcised keep the law; but desire to have you circumcised, that they may glory in your flesh.
> [14] But God forbid that I should glory, save in the cross of our Lord Jesus Christ, by whom the world is crucified unto me, and I unto the world.
> [15] For in Christ Jesus neither circumcision availeth any thing, nor uncircumcision, but a new creature.
> [16] And as many as walk according to this rule, peace be on them, and mercy, and upon the Israel of God. [Galatians 6:12-16]

---

[48] subterfuge noun
1. : Deception used to achieve an end: tried to get her to sign the contract by subterfuge.
2. : A deceptive stratagem or device: The meeting was a subterfuge to get him out of his office while it was searched.
THE FREE DICTIONARY BY FARLEX, 'subterfuge,' accessed 17 January 2023, https://www.thefreedictionary.com/subterfuge.

The Galatians 6 companion passage to Acts 15 essentially appears to interpret the Israelite Law (Torah), for the commandment regarding **circumcision for Gentiles joining Israel** — *to have been nullified!*'

Why do I stress the idea of <u>Gentiles joining Israel</u>?

<u>Simply</u>, <u>because</u> <u>the</u> <u>religion</u> <u>known</u> <u>as</u> CHRISTIANITY *DID NOT EXIST* at <u>the</u> <u>time</u> <u>of</u> <u>the</u> <u>purported</u> <u>original</u> <u>writings</u> <u>of</u> <u>the</u> Christian <u>New</u> <u>Testament</u>!

'Joining Israel,' <u>at</u> <u>that</u> <u>time</u>, would have been tantamount to joining Jews in their religious life!

To me, the Acts 15 passage is especially egregious because it attributes the decision for Gentiles joining themselves to Jewish Israel — *to James and the Apostle Peter* — without evidence of any acknowledgement of the numerous passages in the Jewish Scriptures which expressly define that relationship!

Acts 15:7-21

> 7 And when there had been much disputing, Peter rose up, and said unto them, Men and brethren, ye know how that a good while ago God made choice among us, that the Gentiles by my mouth should hear the word of the gospel, and believe.
> 8 And God, which knoweth the hearts, bare them witness, giving them the Holy Ghost, even as he did unto us;
> 9 And put no difference between us and them, purifying their hearts by faith.

10 Now therefore why tempt ye God, to put a yoke upon the neck of the disciples, which neither our fathers nor we were able to bear?

11 But we believe that through the grace of the Lord Jesus Christ we shall be saved, even as they.

12 Then all the multitude kept silence, and gave audience to Barnabas and Paul, declaring what miracles and wonders God had wrought among the Gentiles by them.

13 And after they had held their peace, James answered, saying, Men and brethren, hearken unto me:

14 Simeon hath declared how God at the first did visit the Gentiles, to take out of them a people for his name.

15 And to this agree the words of the prophets; as it is written,

16 After this I will return, and will build again the tabernacle of David, which is fallen down; and I will build again the ruins thereof, and I will set it up:

17 That the residue of men might seek after the Lord, and all the Gentiles, upon whom my name is called, saith the Lord, who doeth all these things.

18 Known unto God are all his works from the beginning of the world.

19 Wherefore my sentence is, that we trouble not them, which from among the Gentiles are turned to God:

20 But that we write unto them, that they abstain from pollutions of idols, and from fornication, and from things strangled, and from blood.

21 For Moses of old time hath in every city them that preach him, being read in the synagogues every sabbath day.

[Acts 15:7-21]

I believe that it is a travesty that those holding the New Testament as Holy Scripture, **especially followers of Paul and Luke, generally do not verify the integrity of their texts.**

It appears that they just accept those narratives as if they are automatically God–ordained–truth, while giving little credence to alternative views nor having a desire to verify what are easily ascertained to be unfounded claims when comparing their references in the Hebrew-language based Jewish Scriptures!

At the time that the purported events were expressed to have occurred, it is quite likely that a **Jewish audience** would have understood that non-Jews who desired to become part of Israel would have to come along side them in following the Torah!

Unfortunately, 'the Christian Scriptures' labeled those Israelite Jews by the damning moniker of 'Judaizers.'[49] Yet, those Jews would have rightly interpreted the instructions of the written Torah of Yehovah concerning Gentiles joining Israel!

This passage from Acts 15 is deceptive on many levels.

---

[49] Stephen Baker, 'Why Were Judaizers Such Big Problems in the Early Church?,' last modified 10 Feb 2022, https://www.christianity.com/wiki/christian-terms/why-were-judaizers-such-big-problems-in-the-early-church.html.

Luke's narrative purports that the Apostle Peter and James, Jesus' brother, ***properly quoted the Jewish Scripture!*** However, Luke has them rather indirectly ***misquote*** a Jewish Scripture passage from the book of **Amos** and also remove it from the plain meaning of its natural context. If they actually did so, they were breaking the **ninth commandment** themselves!

The passage in the book of Acts infers that Peter and James then used the **out-of-context reference** to support an unscriptural idea which directly **contravenes the Torah** — *that male Gentiles could join Israel without being circumcised* — a direct contravention of the clear requirement written in the Torah of Yehovah as given by the hand of Moses!

This is a subtle deception which has been used frequently by the—self—appointed Apostle Paul. However, here, in Acts 15, Paul's friend, **Luke,** has likewise employed it to blatantly disregard the pertinent Jewish texts easily found on the subject.

Yet, at the same time, in what appears to give him legitimacy, Luke has the authentic Apostle Peter and Jesus's brother James ***misquote*** a passage from the book of Amos; the result of which helps to further **obfuscate the truth in the source!**

In my opinion, this is a just a story, a narrative written by the biographer friend of Paul to help verify Paul's ***antinomian***[50] views. I do not believe that the native Israelites, Peter and James, who were taught directly by Jesus himself, would have totally disregarded the Jewish Scriptures to support *the Gentile Christian doctrine of Paul and Luke — based upon a total rejection of the plain teachings easily found in the Torah.*

---

[50] antinomian noun

1. : one who holds that under the gospel dispensation of grace (see GRACE entry 1 sense 1a (https://www.merriam-webster.com/dictionary/grace#h1)) the moral law is of no use or obligation because faith alone is necessary to salvation
2. : one who rejects a socially established morality
Merriam—Webster Dictionary, 'antinomian,' accessed 16 January 2023, https://www.merriam-webster.com/dictionary/antinomianism.

To properly analyze this, I will quote the passage from Amos, referenced in Acts 15, **in its context**. I believe that will clearly show that **the Amos reference has absolutely nothing to do with circumcision, nor to Gentiles!**

Note that I have underlined the verses which appear to me to be referenced in Acts 15.

10 All the sinners of My people shall die by the sword, that say: 'The evil shall not overtake nor confront us.'
11 In that day will I raise up the tabernacle of David that is fallen, and close up the breaches thereof, and I will raise up his ruins, and I will build it as in the days of old;
12 That they may possess the remnant of Edom, and all the nations, upon whom My name is called, saith Yehovah that doeth this.
13 Behold, the days come, saith Yehovah, that the plowman shall overtake the reaper, and the treader of grapes him that soweth seed; and the mountains shall drop sweet wine, and all the hills shall melt.
14 And I will turn the captivity of My people Israel, and they shall build the waste cities, and inhabit them; and they shall plant vineyards, and drink the wine thereof; they shall also make gardens, and eat the fruit of them.
15 And I will plant them upon their land, and they shall no more be plucked up

out of their land which I have given them, saith Yehovah thy God.
[Amos 9:10-15]

Taking Jewish Scripture out of its natural context is often deployed as a means to justify and authenticate the reasoning for decisions or to try to corroborate views expressed in the Christian Bible, aka the New Testament.

Notably, Luke stresses his attention to detail at the beginning of his books of Luke and Acts. Both preambles are directed to a certain **Theophilus**.[51] Luke expresses or infers <u>that</u> <u>he</u> <u>had</u> <u>reviewed</u> <u>all</u> <u>available</u> <u>living</u> <u>sources</u> <u>for</u> <u>his</u> <u>'meticulous'</u> records.

> 1 Forasmuch as many have taken in hand to set forth in order a declaration of those things which are most surely believed among us,
> 2 Even as they delivered them unto us, which from the beginning were eyewitnesses, and ministers of the word;

---

[51] Theophilus of Antioch
Theophilus (Greek: Θεόφιλος ὁ Ἀντιοχεύς) was Patriarch of Antioch[1] from 169 until 182. He succeeded Eros c. 169, and was succeeded by Maximus I c. 183, according to Henry Fynes Clinton,[2] but these dates are only approximations. His death probably occurred between 183 and 185.[3]

His writings (the only remaining being his apology to Autolycus) indicate that he was born a pagan, not far from the Tigris and Euphrates, and was led to embrace Christianity by studying the Holy Scriptures, especially the prophetical books.[4] He makes no reference to his office in his existing writings, nor is any other fact in his life recorded. Eusebius, however, speaks of the zeal which he and the other chief shepherds displayed in driving away the heretics who were attacking Christ's flock, with special mention of his work against Marcion.[5] He made contributions to the departments of Christian literature, polemics, exegetics, and apologetics. William Sanday [6] describes him as "one of the precursors of that group of writers who, from Irenaeus to Cyprian, not only break the obscurity which rests on the earliest history of the Church, but alike in the East and in the West carry it to the front in literary eminence, and distance all their heathen contemporaries".

From Wikipedia, the free encyclopedia, 'Theophilus of Antioch,' accessed July 2014, http://en.wikipedia.org/wiki/Theophilus_of_Antioch.

³ It seemed good to me also, having had perfect understanding of all things from the very first, to write unto thee in order, most excellent Theophilus,

⁴ That thou mightest know the certainty of those things, wherein thou hast been instructed. [Luke 1:1-4]

¹ The former treatise have I made, O Theophilus, of all that Jesus began both to do and teach, [Acts 1:1]

The result of this <u>subterfuge</u> is that the authoritative source texts of the Jewish Scriptures seemingly **were not considered** in order to corroborate their analysis in Acts 15. I realize that I quoted Luke earlier regarding Theophilus, but because he insisted that he was a true recorder, I have restated it here.

Again, there are numerous passages related to circumcision in the Jewish Scriptures which **<u>apply</u> <u>directly</u> <u>to</u> <u>Gentiles!</u>**

Unfortunately, many believers in **the Christian gospel according to Paul** appear to hold that **his interpretation** is equivalent to that of the Almighty. Therefore, Paul cannot be questioned nor challenged! **<u>So, why should they do so</u>?**

Were they to actually read, with an attempt to understand the authoritative Jewish Scriptures, they could discover the plain and simple meaning of the texts regarding circumcision for non–Jews desiring to join themselves to Jewish Israel!

In my opinion, informed Christians should check references to the Jewish Scriptures based on the Leningrad Codex – _NOT the Septuagint_ – made in the New Testament to ensure that the quotes are <u>accurately represented</u>, that they are <u>true</u>, and that they are <u>in context</u>!

Suffice it to say, that, if quotes of the authoritative Jewish Scriptures are *mispresented by their references* in the Christian New Testament, *sincere readers should be honest* and challenge the belief system promulgated therein!

Shall I remind them that Jesus essentially prophesied that '<u>many</u> <u>will</u> <u>come</u> <u>in</u> <u>my</u> <u>name</u>, <u>saying</u>, <u>I</u> <u>am</u> <u>Christ</u>, <u>and</u> <u>shall</u> <u>deceive</u> <u>many</u>.'

And, of such, was *Paul* – *false prophet and false Apostle!*

So, What Do The Authoritative Jewish Scriptures Actually Say?

From the first instance, in the Jewish Scriptures, regarding *circumcision of non–Jews,* it is abundantly clear that **Yehovah – Elohim, <u>the</u> <u>God</u> <u>of</u> <u>the</u> <u>real</u> <u>Jews</u>,** gave explicit instructions:

> **48 And when a stranger shall sojourn with thee, and will keep the passover to the LORD, let all his males be circumcised, and then let him come near and keep it; and he shall be as one that is born in the land; but no uncircumcised person shall eat thereof.**
>
> **49 One Torah shall be to him that is homeborn, and unto the stranger that sojourneth among you.**
> [Exodus 12:48-49]

Those Who Join Natural Israel: '<u>The</u> <u>Strangers</u> <u>Among</u> <u>You</u>

— *Must Also Follow The Torah!*'

It is quite evident from the **authority of the Jewish Scriptures** that non-Jews who join themselves to Israel *must also observe the same commandments and statutes given to those Israelites they dwell amongst.*

⁴⁹ One Torah shall be to him that is homeborn, and unto the stranger that sojourneth among you. [Exodus 12:49]

Thus, if a non-Jew believes that he or she is now part of Israel, *even as a consequence of a belief system based upon the notion that Jesus is the Jewish Messiah,* it is quite clear from the Jewish Scriptures that they must likewise follow the Torah that Yehovah (God) gave to Israel by the hand of Moses!

Yet, many Christians have embraced the idea that even *spurious* Christian Scriptures have somehow superseded the authoritative, Hebrew-language based Jewish Scriptures!

In other words, *many Christians act as if they have a God–ordained license to misinterpret, misrepresent and misquote, to take out–of–context — the plain meaning as found in the authoritative Jewish Scriptures.*

As I understand it, a great many Christians who arrogantly believe that they are somehow now *The Israel of God, will not* even consider that the commandments found in the Torah should apply to them. **Yet, the many of them naturally consider that *promises* directed to Israel do apply to them,** and even that 'The Ten Commandments' apply to all people!

Paul's Mysterious Doctrine, 'Salvation by Grace'

I believe that their reasoning is a direct consequence from following the teachings of their *'false prophet, the self–*

appointed Apostle Paul,' essentially based upon **his seminal teaching "...you are not under the law (the Torah)":**

> ¹⁴ For sin shall not have dominion over you: for ye are not under the law, but under grace. [Romans 6:14]

A Definition of Grace:

a : unmerited divine assistance given to humans for their regeneration or sanctification
b : a virtue coming from God
c : a state of sanctification enjoyed through divine assistance[52]

Romans 6:14 is the culmination of Paul's mysterious doctrine describing the relationship of the Christian based upon a belief in the occurrence of the death and resurrection of Jesus, **_whereby the belief/thinking itself in the resurrection of Jesus transports a person out of the realm of a natural human birth into a supernatural one._** Do their actions matter?

Is it at all possible, as I described earlier, that the visions and revelations of the self-identifying, 'resurrected Jesus,' by Paul, were actually from **false, demonic, lying spirits, ghosts, familiar spirits** – *calling themselves 'Jesus?'*

If that is so, is it not also possible that **ideas** of merely having a belief in Paul's **demonic, familiar spirit friend,** identifying himself as Jesus Christ — **that belief transports a person into a supernatural birth?** **If so, is it at all possible that, perhaps, that idea may also be *demonic*?**

---

[52] grace, Merriam–Webster Dictionary, accessed 9 Dec 2022, https://www.merriam-webster.com. com/dictionary/grace.

It certainly appears that followers of Paul believe that the written Torah of Yehovah does not apply to them, **yet** **the** **positive** **promises** **to** **Israel** **are** **their** **own** **particular** **inheritance**!

Because our Western culture is rooted in what is thought to be a Judeo–Christian ethic, that way of thinking actually does not seem so foreign to many! Thus, followers of Paul typically do not question their beliefs or verify the **source references which supposedly authenticate those beliefs.**

Should these things tacitly define those 'Pauline Christians' as belonging to a cult? **In actuality, they are following a lying, familiar spirit or ghost** — *a* ***DEMON*** — since they have embraced the deceptive doctrines and teachings of a false prophet – the false Apostle Paul!

It is apparent that followers of Paul are typically unwilling to challenge, for validity, what they consider to be the preeminent and true Holy Scriptures, their own New Testament sources!

Simply, some act as though they cannot imagine nor consider any other system of belief as having any legitimacy! Many believe that the New Testament gives the real interpretation for the Jewish Scriptures! Does this abject arrogance give them a license to believe that they, alone, are the True Israel of God?

Of course, a subject which is especially egregious to many calling themselves 'Christian' is that, in joining Israel, their **males must be circumcised** — but, that even they must also honor Holy laws of the Torah, including prescribed **food laws!**

Would that necessarily mean that eating things that they have grown to love should also be forbidden, such as **pig** and **shellfish** – like bacon, ham, shrimp and lobster (could they give those things up for Jesus)? Should they also be subject to observing each and every one of the Ten Commandments, not the least of which is to observe the seventh day Sabbath?

Obviously, those things are for the most part what many might consider to be anathema![53] **Yet, haven't they been told that the Jewish Jesus is presumed to have observed the commandments and statutes of the Torah?**

Would it also mean they could not retain their idols or other devoted objects of worship? Didn't their prophet, Paul, make it clear that *'you were carried away unto these dumb idols,...?'*[54]

Obviously, I may be putting words in their mouths, **but are not these things some _'food for thought?'_**

Are Christians Now The Israel of God?*

*Because many sing Holy, Holy, Holy
Holy, Holy, Holy.
They sing Holy, Holy, Holy
— _With PIG between their teeth!_

---

[53] anathema | əˈnaTHəmə |
noun
1 something or someone that one vehemently dislikes: racial hatred was anathema to her.
2 a formal curse by a pope or a council of the Church, excommunicating a person or denouncing a doctrine.
• literary a strong curse: the sergeant clutched the ruined communicator, muttering anathemas.
ORIGIN
early 16th century: from ecclesiastical Latin, 'excommunicated person, excommunication', from Greek anathema 'thing dedicated', (later) 'thing devoted to evil, accursed thing', from anatithenai 'to set up'.
Dictionary, version 2.2.2 (203.1) Copyright 2005-1017 Apple Inc.
[54] 2 Ye know that ye were Gentiles, carried away unto these dumb idols, even as ye were led. 1 Corinthians 12:2.

The Talmudic Deception

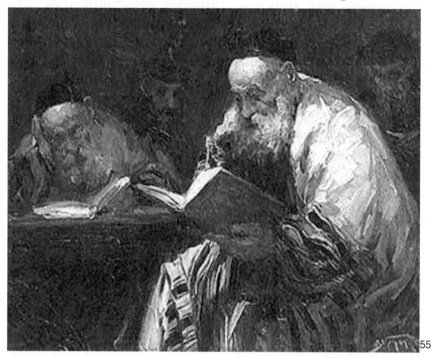

55

I get it; most people want to be accepted. This can easily be seen as young children will often act-out in a certain way when trying to get their parents' attention for approval. As adults, we may also look for acceptance, especially by those who we may consider to be *the authoritative leaders.*

Many who want to have a better understanding of **'things–Jewish'** will often seek what is considered to be the Jewish authority for acceptance. Most of the time, that ends up being Jewish *rabbinic* authorities; in essence, rabbis who hold to the authority of the Talmud.[56]

---

[55] By Adolf Behrman (1876 – 1942) - Zbiory ŻIH (Żydowski Instytut Historyczny), Public Domain, https://commons.wikimedia.org/w/index.php?curid=20753920. Converted to grayscale and image posterization applied.

[56] The Talmud is the textual record of generations of rabbinic debate about law, philosophy, and biblical interpretation, compiled between the 3rd and 8th centuries and structured as

I believe that there is **an overall misunderstanding** of people who have had little involvement with the Talmudic community to somehow **buy into the rabbinic argument that _true Judaism_** is only found through the Jewish rabbis (Talmudists).

Talmudists base the idea that they, alone, are the only Jewish authority upon an <u>out-of-context</u> <u>Scriptural reference</u> which they use as validation for that authority!

In doing so, they absolutely misquote Exodus 23:2, discarding the plain meaning of its context; they render it to say, to the effect, that _**all Jews must incline after the majority.**_[57]

As I understand it, since **<u>they</u> <u>believe</u> <u>that</u> <u>they</u> <u>are</u>** _'that majority,'_ they necessarily expect that all Jews must submit to their rabbinic authority! Yet, if the passage was quoted as written, it could not possibly be interpreted as they have done.

I will let you, the reader, decide whether or not the Talmudist rabbinic interpretation is cogent or rather that it is spurious. If you find their claims to be false, then I would ask that you **not be afraid of them, because, like Saul of Tarsus – Paul – who was also <u>self</u>-appointed, _they should absolutely be considered to be false prophets_**!

The Exodus 23:2 passage in Hebrew and English will follow below. I quote from Exodus 23:1-3, so it provides the context:

---

commentary on the Mishnah with stories interwoven. The Talmud exists in two versions: the more commonly studied Babylonian Talmud was compiled in present-day Iraq, while the Jerusalem Talmud was compiled in Israel.
Talmud Babylonian, The William Davidson Edition, accessed 1 Feb 2023, https://www.sefaria.org/texts/Talmud.
[57] Daniel Roth, "'Go according to the majority' - But first know the 49 vs 49" [Parashat Mishpatim],' Elmad Pardes Digital Library, posted 3 Nov 2016, https://elmad.pardes.org/2016/11/go-according-to-the-majority-but-first-know-the-49-vs-49-parashat-mishpatim/.

א לֹא תִשָּׂא שֵׁמַע שָׁוְא אַל־תָּשֶׁת יָדְךָ
עִם־רָשָׁע לִהְיֹת עֵד חָמָס:
ב לֹא־תִהְיֶה אַחֲרֵי־רַבִּים לְרָעֹת וְלֹא־
תַעֲנֶה עַל־רִב לִנְטֹת אַחֲרֵי רַבִּים
לְהַטֹּת:
ג וְדָל לֹא תֶהְדַּר בְּרִיבוֹ:

¹ Thou shalt not utter a false report; put not thy hand with the wicked to be an unrighteous witness.
² Thou shalt not follow a multitude to do evil; neither shalt thou bear witness in a cause to turn aside after a multitude to pervert justice;
³ neither shalt thou favour a poor man in his cause. [Exodus 23:1-3]

Verse 2 of Exodus 23 is the full verse that the rabbis just 'take a part of' completely out-of-context, and *remove its negation.*

Any thinking person should easily see that the verse **does not say**, 'Thou shalt follow after a majority.' Rather, it clearly states that **you must NOT follow a multitude [majority] *to do evil*** and that **you should NOT bear a [false] witness** to turn a multitude **to pervert justice!** Here is verse 2, again:

² Thou shalt not follow a multitude to do evil; neither shalt thou bear witness in a cause to turn aside after a multitude to pervert justice;

Unfortunately, this practice of **altering the written Holy Scriptures,** by just taking pieces of a verse to mean something completely different than the in-context original, is not uncommon among Talmudists, rabbis. I do not believe that they consider the written Torah as authoritative, sanctified and Holy!

Moreover, I have stated elsewhere that rabbis, as a group, act as if they are the de facto Elohim/God! They certainly demand that their own edicts must be followed as if they are divine law!

Saying that the Talmudists are the de facto authority for all things *Jewish* is like saying that the Roman Catholic Church is the de facto authority for all things *Christian*.

No doubt but **many Protestants** would absolutely object to that statement; they would rather say that the Holy Scriptures are their authority, rather than the *'Roman Catholic abomination!'*

Thus, even when Gentiles are exposed to such Talmudic groups like **'Jews for Judaism,'** in accepting arguments regarding the fallacies of Christianity, many of them will leave off their previous ties and actually convert to *Talmudic* Judaism.

Likewise, within Messianic Jewish[58] circles there are some groups that hold onto a form of Talmudic Judaism, usually sprinkled with what I might call 'Jesus-isms' or 'Yeshua-bites!'

I stressed, in a previous chapter, about the requirement in the Torah that Gentiles who want to join Israel must be circumcised. Ironically, ***Messianic*** assemblies often have more Gentile members than Jewish, and even some don't have any Jewish people at all as part of their congregations!

I said, ironically, because for a non-Jew to *join themselves to Israel,* quite naturally they must dwell among Jews (Israel)!

---

[58] Tamar Fox, 'Who Are Messianic "Jews"? These Christians observe some Jewish practices, but the major Jewish denominations do not recognize their faith as a form of Judaism.", accessed 14 February 2023, https://www.myjewishlearning.com/article/messianic-judaism/.

In conversations with some non-Jewish people concerning the idea of getting circumcised, I have often heard them express **a belief that they are somehow already circumcised —** *in **a** **spiritual** **sense*** **— through their faith in Jesus!**

In the same way, there is often a belief among them that they are somehow now ***'Spiritual Israel'*** as well.

There is a movement, within Judaism as well as in Messianic Jewish circles, that refers to themselves as *Torah Observant.* However, the term *Torah Observant* **is a huge deception!**

"Torah Observant" — Actually Means *Observant of the ORAL Torah!*

In reality, those who call themselves *Torah Observant* actually are adherents to **Talmudic Judaism.** They wear prayer shawls and head coverings (called kippot, pronounced ki-pote; plural of kippah, or otherwise known as Yarmulkes). They may don tefillin (phylacteries) while reading the morning set of prayers as defined in rabbinic prayer books, etc.

Torah Observant for these people is a **misnomer** as **most who hear that term** will typically think of the *written* Torah (the five books of Moses) instead!

Unfortunately, those calling themselves **Torah Observant** are actually adhering to what is called **the Oral Torah**, a system of teachings whereby rabbis have insisted that there was always a parallel **Oral Torah** passed along (to a secret group) with that which was written (not so secret).

They will tell you that the **Oral Torah** fills in the gaps where the **written Torah** may be silent, *as in how to ritually slaughter an animal prior to offering it as a sacrifice.*

So, when they say, **Torah Observant,** they really mean 'practicing the teachings of the **Oral tradition'** rather than what many people understand to be the Torah written by Moses! They also give greater authority to the **Oral Torah!**

But there's another Torah, known as the Oral Torah — or Torah she-ba'al peh. The Oral Torah refers to the later works of the rabbinic period — most prominently the Mishnah and the Gemara, jointly known as the Talmud — that explain and expound upon the statutes recorded in the Written Torah. The traditional Jewish view is that both these Torah's were revealed at Mount Sinai, but the Oral Torah was passed down as oral tradition (hence the name) until the destruction of the Second Temple in the early part of the Common Era, when fear of it being lost forever led to it being committed to writing for the first time.

The classic statement of the authority of the Oral Torah is found in the first mishnah in Avot 1:1: "Moses received the Torah at Sinai and transmitted it to Joshua, Joshua to the elders, and the elders to the prophets, and the prophets to the Men of the Great Assembly." This statement was meant to establish that the traditions practiced during the time of the Mishnah were not human creations, but traced their authority back to Sinai. In the Middle Ages, Maimonides stated this quite explicitly in his Introduction to the Mishnah:

Know that each commandment that the Holy One, blessed be He, gave to Moshe, our teacher – peace be upon him – was given to him with its explanation. He would say to him the commandment and afterward tell him its explanation and content; and [so too with] everything that is included in the Book of the Torah.

The Oral Torah is crucial to the normative practice of Judaism today. The prescriptions for daily life found in the Bible are typically cryptic, vague, and even contradictory. Some are completely indecipherable on their own. The Oral Law expounds at great length on these sources, providing a vast literature that translates scriptural sources into a guide for daily living.[59]

Again, **Torah Observant** to these folks means practicing Judaism according to Talmudic, rabbinic edicts, found in the so-called **Oral Torah**, instead of strictly following the actual **written Torah of Moses and giving it the preeminence!**

Have you ever wondered whether the rabbinic Jewish religion known to us all today is the same Judaism which was practiced in biblical times, in the time of Moses and the prophets?

For the past 2000 years, the common term "Torah observant", regarding the Torah or the commandments, hasn't really meant what most people think it means. Nowadays, it is simply impossible to keep the commandments of the Torah, as they revolve around the Temple, the Tabernacle, the priesthood, the altar and the heart of it all: Sacrificing offerings to atone for our sins. This has all ceased to exist since the destruction of the Temple, 2000 years ago. Today, the expression "Torah observant", represents people who follow rabbinic rules.

---

[59] My Jewish Learning, 'The Written Torah and the Oral Torah,' accessed 19 Feb 2023, https://www.myjewishlearning.com/article/the-formation-of-the-oral-torah/.

There is almost no connection to Moses and his original commandments anymore.

Truth be told, the rabbis have played the most sophisticated scheme on the nation of Israel: They made us all think that rabbinic rules and traditions, which were invented by them, are in fact "the Law of Moses". In the next few minutes, we are going to prove to you that the Law of Moses and the rabbinic law have nothing to do with one another and that the "Oral Law" was never given by God on Mount Sinai, but that it is nothing more than urban legend.[60]

Actually, if I were to try to give a logical comparison to illustrate *Oral Torah,* I would say that **Saul of Tarsus (the Christian Apostle Paul)**, who, in fact is reported to have declared that he had been a Pharisee (followers of the *Oral Tradition* in the time of Jesus) is a great example with which to compare.

Paul claimed to have had visions when there were no others to corroborate them but himself. Moreover, he did so following the manner of the **warning by Jesus himself:**

> [3] And as he sat upon the mount of Olives, the disciples came unto him privately, saying, Tell us, when shall these things be? and what shall be the sign of thy coming, and of the end of the world?
> [4] And Jesus answered and said unto them, Take heed that no man deceive you.
> [5] For many shall come in my name, saying, I am Christ; and shall deceive many. [Matthew 24:3-5]

---

[60] One For Israel, 'DID GOD REALLY GIVE AN "ORAL LAW" AT SINAI? (RABBINIC ORAL LAW DEBUNKED),' last modified 30 May 2016, https://www.oneforisrael.org/bible-based-teaching-from-israel/did-god-also-give-moses-an-oral-law/.

Similarly, **there is no way to corroborate the claims of Talmudists** that there was ever an ancient *oral tradition* **just because they claim it so.** They simply declare that these originally unwritten laws were passed down through Jewish history by one-on-one contact to a **_secret_**, **_privileged_** **_group_**.

A Lie, Believed By Many, Does Not Make It True!

Had an *Oral Torah* actually existed when Ezra and Nehemiah restored the Jewish state after exile in Babylon, most certainly they would have given some allusion to it in their writings.

But, as in the entire Jewish Scriptures, there was silence.

Nowhere in the entire authoritative Jewish Scriptures is there any evidence or allusion that an Oral Tradition system ever existed! For it to be held in such prominence by rabbis, shouldn't the written Jewish Scriptures have even acknowledged it?

Again, the Written Torah is silent regarding any Oral Torah!

Rabbinic 'Noahide Laws' — Only Gentiles Need Apply!

I find it quite unfortunate that Jewish, rabbinic authorities, have contributed to the overall misunderstanding of non–Jewish people regarding observance of the Law (Torah) of Yehovah.

How is that, you may ask?

By what appears to minimize the relevance of the written Torah, in their own writings rabbis have introduced *a different set of laws pertaining to Gentiles.*

They refer to them as **'The Seven Noahide Laws.'**[61]

Of course, in their explanations, they will say that these seven laws pertain to everyone, but in practice most people that know about these declarations expect that they are directed to Gentiles and a separate set of laws pertain to Jews.

However, neither do they seem to acknowledge that non–Jews can actually become part of Israel but that they must observe these separate laws of division (even though they have established a conversion process for those wishing to join officially).

In my opinion, introducing this creative concept for how non–Jews can have a relationship with the God of Israel; taking part, yet, still as outsiders, in the wider Jewish religious community — is part of an intentional deception against those people!

Please, allow me to explain.

As a Karaite[62] (Jewish Scripturalist), I believe the passage from Exodus 12:49, ***"One Torah shall be to him that is homeborn, and unto the stranger that sojourneth among you."*** has greater bearing upon interpreting how non–Jews should be related to the Torah of Yehovah than the 'unscriptural (**i.e., not based upon the written Torah**) rabbinic

---

[61] Chabad.org, 'The 7 Noahide Laws: Universal Morality', accessed 12 January 2023. 2023, https://www.chabad.org/library/article_cdo/aid/62221/jewish/The-7-Noahide-Laws-Universal-Morality.htm.

[62] 'Karaism is the original form of Judaism commanded by God to the Jewish people in the Torah. Karaites accept the Tanakh (Jewish Bible) as the word of God and as the sole religious authority. At the same time, Karaites deny human additions to the Torah such as the Rabbinic Oral Law because Deuteronomy 4:2 states, "You shall not add to the word which I have commanded you, neither shall you diminish from it..." Karaite Judaism also rejects the Rabbinical principle that the Rabbis are the sole authorities for interpreting the Bible.' Shawn Lichaa, Nehemia Gordon, Meir Rekhavi, "As It Is Written A Brief Case For Karaism," (Hilkiah Press, 2006), p7. Reproduced by permission.

edicts' (תַּקָּנוֹת takkanot[63]) <u>which</u> <u>rabbis</u> <u>insist</u> <u>must</u> <u>be</u> <u>followed</u>, <u>just</u> <u>as</u> <u>if</u> <u>they</u> <u>are</u> <u>divinely</u> <u>inspired</u> <u>law</u>, <u>as</u> <u>if</u> <u>they</u> <u>are</u> <u>directly</u> <u>the</u> <u>words</u> <u>of</u> <u>Almighty</u> <u>God</u>!

Unlike what is often assumed, the **'Seven Noahide Laws'** do not exist as a singularly defined unit in the Jewish Scriptures!

Although some of these laws are taken from the section known as the Ten Commandments (Exodus 20, Deuteronomy 5), as a group they are totally made–up by rabbis, whose inspiration is directed by the Talmud.[64] I often refer to rabbis simply as Talmudists, or more descriptively, Talmudic rabbis.

I find a certain irony in that many evangelical Christians would easily say that 'Jewish Law' as well as the 'rabbinic belief system' are based solely upon the words–of–man, but their own 'belief system' is based solely upon the words-of-God!

What I consider to be actual words of God are the Hebrew–language based Jewish Scriptures found in the ancient, Hebrew-language source known as the Leningrad Codex.

I consider to be mere words-of-man those instances, and their misinterpretations, of supposed Jewish Scriptures that have been taken out of their natural context and/or misquoted in the Christian Bible, aka The New Testament!

Similarly, rabbinic Talmudists also take the written Jewish Scriptures out of their natural context and often misquote them, the end result being that **they base their own set of laws in that same deceptive manner as do** *'Pauline Christians.'*

---

[63] A takkanah (Heb. תַּקָּנוֹת pl.; sing. תַּקָּנָה) is a directive enacted by the halakhic scholars, or other competent body (see *Takkanot ha-Kahal), enjoying the force of law. It constitutes one of the legal sources of Jewish law (see *Mishpat Ivri). Jewish Virtual Library, 'Takkanah,' accessed 19 May 2022, https://www.jewishvirtuallibrary.org/takkanah.
[64] My Jewish Learning, 'What Is the Talmud? An intergenerational rabbinic conversation that is studied, not read.', accessed 16 Jan 2023, https://www.myjewishlearning.com/article/talmud-101/.

Adding confusion to this milieu is that Talmudists have divided the actual Word-of-God, known as the Torah, into that which was **written by Moses** and that which they believe was passed down from Moses by word-of-mouth, **the Oral Tradition.** Ironically, they hold that the **Oral Tradition** has a greater claim to legitimate authority than that which was written by Moses!

> Rabbi Aryeh Kaplan wrote on this subject: 'In many respects, the Oral Torah is **more important than the Written Torah.** It is a foundation of our faith to believe that God gave Moses an oral explanation of the Torah along with the written text. This oral tradition is now essentially preserved in the Talmud and Midrashim. We thus speak of two Torah's. There is the Written Torah (Torah SheBiKetav) and the Oral Torah (Torah SheB'Al Peh). Both are alluded to in God's statement to Moses, "Come up to Me to the mountain, and I will give you… the Torah and the commandments" (Exodus 24:12). http://www.aish.com/jl/b/ol/48943186.html

> The Talmud claims that God made His covenant with Israel on the basis of the Written Law and the Oral Law: 'The Holy One, Blessed be He, did not make His covenant with Israel except by virtue of the Oral Law.' Gittin 60B.[65]

More Confusion:
The Myth Of The 613 Commandments!

---

[65] Tony Pierce, 'Was there an Oral Torah given at Sinai?,' The Messiah Factor, accessed 19 Feb 2023, https://messiahfactor.com/was-there-an-oral-torah-given-at-sinai/.

'GARTI' — גַּ֫רְתִּי

ג = 3

ר = 200

ת = 400

י = 10

613

וַיְצַ֣ו אֹתָם֮ לֵאמֹר֒ כֹּ֣ה תֹאמְר֔וּן לַֽאדֹנִ֖י לְעֵשָׂ֑ו כֹּ֤ה אָמַר֙
עַבְדְּךָ֣ יַֽעֲקֹ֔ב עִם־לָבָ֣ן גַּ֔רְתִּי וָֽאֵחַ֖ר עַד־עָֽתָּה׃

5 And he commanded them, saying: 'Thus shall ye say unto my lord Esau: Thus saith thy servant Jacob: I have sojourned with Laban, and stayed until now. [Genesis 32:5]

'The 613 Commandments' is a <u>myth</u> promulgated within rabbinic Judaism. Like so many of their other dictates, using this terminology without giving any list, Scriptural reference, explanation or definition to coincide with their messaging, <u>they have</u> <u>obtained</u> a <u>certain</u> <u>power</u>, which is no doubt the result of expressing a **secret knowledge unavailable to outsiders.**

So, you might rightly ask, **"Just what are the 613 Commandments supposed to be about?"** The answer comes from breaking down how the idea of the 613 Commandments was created. There is a term bantered about in Jewish circles, mostly by Talmudists, called gematria. The word, gematria, simply means "geometry or mathematics."

I found an exchange with Nehemia Gordon and a host on a podcast which provides a very good explanation for **'the 613!'**

> **Nehemia:** Okay. So, this idea of 613 commandments is actually something that I was taught very young. I mean, definitely before I could drink or drive, I must have been seven or eight years old, maybe earlier. One of my earliest memories is being taught about the 613 commandments as a fact, and I remember studying when I was a child in school, we were studying in the Book of Genesis in chapter 32 verse 5. There, Jacob is meeting with Esav, Esau, his brother. He's been away for about 20 years. He's been over in Aramea, in what today is Iraq, living with Laban. And when he introduces himself to Esav, to Esau, he says, "Thus says your servant, Jacob, 'I have lived with Laban and been delayed until now.'" And the way any normal person would read that is, he's just giving over the facts. But when the rabbis looked at this, they said, "Okay, there's a hidden message here." And the hidden message is in the word "I lived". In Hebrew, "I lived" is one single word, the word "garti."
>
> And what they did is, they took that word and they said, "What's the numerological value of the word 'garti', 'I lived'"? And that's actually an idea that comes from Greek, it's called "gematria". In Hebrew, it's called "gematria". Now, gematria is not actually an authentic Hebrew word. Gematria is simply the Hebrew form of the word "geometry", which was the Greek word for, essentially, "mathematics".
>
> **Don:** Right.

Nehemia: So, based on this Greek idea that you can take letters and make them have equivalent values of numbers, the gematria of the word "I lived" is 613. And the rabbis understood Jacob's statement to Esav to say that, "When I was with Laban, I kept all of the 613 commandments." And this is actually a core doctrine in Rabbinical Judaism, one of probably the big differences with the Karaite approach, the rabbis say that the forefathers going all the way back to Noah, and according to one opinion, all the way back to Adam, had all 613 commandments – meaning, everything a Jew is required to do today, all of the forefathers knew that.[66]

I find it quite unfortunate that many people have been deceived by Talmudic rhetoric, but also, Talmudic rabbis appear to demand that others consider them as the ultimate authority for anything having to do with Judaism — Jewish faith!

I prefer to weigh ideas regarding anything Jewish to be done so by trying to understand the written Jewish Scriptures in the plain meaning found in their immediate context!

בּ לֹא־תִהְיֶ֥ה אַחֲרֵי־רַבִּ֖ים לְרָעֹ֑ת וְלֹא־תַעֲנֶ֣ה
עַל־רִ֗ב לִנְטֹ֛ת אַחֲרֵ֥י רַבִּ֖ים לְהַטֹּֽת׃

2 Thou shalt not follow a multitude to do evil; neither shalt thou bear witness in a cause to turn aside after a multitude to pervert justice; [Exodus 23:2]

---

[66] Nehemia Gordon, "Hebrew Voices #131 - Are There 613 Commandments,", accessed 12 Jan 2023, https://www.nehemiaswall.com/are-there-613-commandments. See 'Transcript.'

The Talmudic Deception

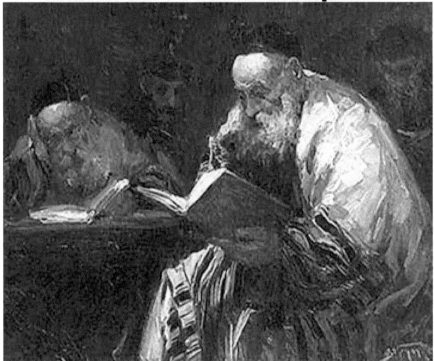

By Adolf Behrman (1876 – 1942) - Zbiory ŻIH (Żydowski Instytut Historyczny), Public Domain,
https://commons.wikimedia.org/w/index.php?curid=20753920

What About The Resurrection?

67

Of all the teachings of Christianity, no doctrine is more central than the bodily resurrection of Jesus Christ from the dead. The truth of the resurrection has been attacked from every angle. New books and television media regularly appear questioning the resurrection, re-hashing old theories about what happened to Jesus' body. Since the resurrection is crucial to Christianity, Christians ought to

---

67 Kat Smith, 'Shallow Focus Photography of White Sheep on Green Grass,' accessed 6 Apr 2023, https://www.pexels.com/photo/shallow-focus-photography-of-white-sheep-on-green-grass-678448/. Converted to grayscale and image posterization applied.

be able to give answers to these inevitable questions with proof and evidence.

The Gospel Accounts of the Resurrection

The first step in defending the resurrection from its detractors is to establish the fact of the historical events that took place as conveyed in the Gospels. As philosopher William Lane Craig notes in his book Reasonable Faith, "The issue is whether the gospel narratives are historically credible accounts or unhistorical legends."[68]

That quote is probably typical of many views from a Christian standpoint regarding the resurrection of Jesus.

The Best Documented Event In History?

Many have stated that **the resurrection of Jesus is the best documented event in all of human history!** Interestingly, the only places where the accounts are documented are within the Christian Scriptures themselves.

From what I have been able to discern, except in Christian writings, the first century of the common era has not provided us with credible evidence that the resurrection event transpired.

---

[68] Justin Holcomb, 'What is the Proof and Evidence of the Resurrection of Jesus Christ?,' Christianity.com, last modified 19 Mar 2021, https://www.christianity.com/jesus/death-and-resurrection/resurrection/what-proof-is-there-of-the-resurrection-of-jesus.html.

For such an important event to Christians, I would think that the surviving written accounts would provide substantial internal evidence **and that any accounts would be in agreement!**

However, in each of the four New Testament narratives, no two agree on the purported story! Some have similarities but none totally agree! **For it to be 'the best documented event in history of the world,' I would want to assume that those who recorded the event could get their stories straight!**

> We know the historical Jesus mainly through four different accounts known as the gospels— Matthew, Mark, Luke, and John—not written hundreds of years later, but within a generation or two of Jesus's life. Apostles Matthew and John provide eyewitness accounts from their years of walking with Jesus as disciples. Mark also had eyewitness experience, although he was only a teenager when Jesus began his public ministry. Luke, the doctor, learned about Jesus from his friend Paul, the apostle who wrote the most letters in the New Testament.[69]

Another Christian organization, Moody Bible Institute, provides the following information for their views on the Resurrection:

THE RESURRECTION OF JESUS CHRIST

> The resurrection of Jesus Christ is the cornerstone of our Christian faith.[1] This event, which occurred almost two thousand years ago, is the best attested fact in human history and experience. The resurrection of Christ was

---

[69]   Scott Powell, 'Jesus Christ's Resurrection Is Probably The Best-Documented Historical Event Ever,' The Federalist A Division Of Fdrlst Media, last modified 15 April 2022, https://thefederalist.com/2022/04/15/jesus-christs-resurrection-is-probably-the-best-documented-historical-event-ever/.

predicted in the Old Testament and by Christ Himself.[2] During the forty days following His resurrection, Jesus showed Himself to be alive from the dead by "many infallible proofs."[3] He appeared at various times and places to many people who told others what they had seen.[4]

Christ's resurrection has been at the heart of the church's message from the Day of Pentecost to the present. By rising from the dead, Jesus Christ demonstrated that He had cleansed the guilt of our past and is able to help us in our present lives.[5] His resurrection assures us that our future is safe and secure.[6] Without Christ's resurrection we would have no salvation from sin, and no hope for our own future resurrection.

The empty tomb is proof of Christ's deity.[7] It guarantees the future resurrection of believers.[8] The resurrection of Christ also provides believers with spiritual power today.[9] The bodily resurrection of Jesus Christ is evidence that God will one day judge the world in righteousness.[10] [70]

[1] 1 Corinthians 15:17
[2] Job 19:25–27; Psalms 16:9–11; 22:22; 118:22–24; Matthew 16:21; Mark 9:30–32; Luke 18:31–34; John 2:19–22
[3] Acts 1:3
[4] Luke 24:33–43; John 20:24–29; 1 Corinthians 15:3–8
[5] Romans 4:24–25; Hebrews 7:25
[6] John 14:19
[7] John 5:26; Romans 1:4
[8] John 14:19; 1 Corinthians 15:20–23
[9] Romans 6:3–4; Ephesians 1:19–21
[10] Acts 17:31

---

[70] Moody Bible Institute, 'THE RESURRECTION OF JESUS CHRIST,' accessed 6 Apr 2023, https://www.moodybible.org/beliefs/positional-statements/resurrection/.

I encourage you to examine the Moody Institute article references to determine if they give absolute hard and incontrovertible evidence as to the resurrection of Jesus.

Their only references to the Jewish Scriptures are from the 2nd footnote: Job 19:25-27; Psalms 16:9-11; 22:22; 118:22-24.

The English translations for those Jewish Scripture verses will hopefully show whether or not they are truly prophetic regarding the **'most attested historical event in all of human history,'** **the resurrection of Jesus Christ:**

25 But as for me, I know that my Redeemer liveth, and that He will witness at the last upon the dust;
26 And when after my skin this is destroyed, then without my flesh shall I see God;
27 Whom I, even I, shall see for myself, and mine eyes shall behold, and not another's. My reins are consumed within me. [Job 19:25-27]

9 Therefore my heart is glad, and my glory rejoiceth; my flesh also dwelleth in safety;
10 For Thou wilt not abandon my soul to the nether-world; neither wilt Thou suffer Thy godly one to see the pit.
11 Thou makest me to know the path of life; in Thy presence is fulness of joy, in Thy right hand bliss for evermore.
[Psalms 16:9-11]

21 Deliver my soul from the sword; mine only one from the power of the dog.
22 Save me from the lion's mouth; yea, from the horns of the wild-oxen do Thou answer me. [Psalms 22:21-22]

22 The stone which the builders rejected is become the chief corner-stone.
23 This is Yehovah's doing; it is marvellous in our eyes.
24 This is the day which Yehovah hath made; we will rejoice and be glad in it.
[Psalms 118:22-24]

To reference the Jewish Scriptures as a means to show *incontrovertible evidence* that those passages absolutely foretell the resurrection of Jesus Christ is simply reading into the text and not looking at the Scripture in its plain meaning and context. **Again, this New Testament event is purported to be the most attested historical event in the history of mankind,** and yet, its references to the Jewish Scriptures, as verification and validation, are just not very convincing, IMHO!

Do any of those Jewish Scripture references **absolutely** point to the death and resurrection of the man, Jesus of Nazareth?
Are we left to be convinced, then, by the descriptions in the New Testament for the great attestation of this important event?

In order to be thorough, I feel that I must provide the accounts of the resurrection of Jesus as found in the four Gospels from the New Testament.

I do not wish to overwhelm you with too much reading. However, this is supposed to be Christian **evidence** of the most attested, best described event in the history of mankind!

If you wish to look up the passages separately in a version you might prefer, the reference passages are Matthew 28:1-20; Mark 16:1-20; Luke 24:1-53 and John 27:1-31, 28:1-14.

Again, I encourage you to read each of the Gospel narratives for the resurrection of Jesus to determine **if the accounts are in complete agreement, <u>especially</u> <u>about</u> <u>the</u> <u>ascension,</u>** or if they are each different and disparate in describing the supposed, most attested event in all of human history!

Matthew 28:1-20

¹ In the end of the sabbath, as it began to dawn toward the first day of the week, came Mary Magdalene and the other Mary to see the sepulchre.

² And, behold, there was a great earthquake: for the angel of the Lord descended from heaven, and came and rolled back the stone from the door, and sat upon it.

³ His countenance was like lightning, and his raiment white as snow:

⁴ And for fear of him the keepers did shake, and became as dead men.

⁵ And the angel answered and said unto the women, Fear not ye: for I know that ye seek Jesus, which was crucified.

⁶ He is not here: for he is risen, as he said. Come, see the place where the Lord lay.

⁷ And go quickly, and tell his disciples that he is risen from the dead; and, behold, he goeth before you into Galilee; there shall ye see him: lo, I have told you.

8 And they departed quickly from the sepulchre with fear and great joy; and did run to bring his disciples word.

9 And as they went to tell his disciples, behold, Jesus met them, saying, All hail. And they came and held him by the feet, and worshipped him.

10 Then said Jesus unto them, Be not afraid: go tell my brethren that they go into Galilee, and there shall they see me.

11 Now when they were going, behold, some of the watch came into the city, and shewed unto the chief priests all the things that were done.

12 And when they were assembled with the elders, and had taken counsel, they gave large money unto the soldiers,

13 Saying, Say ye, His disciples came by night, and stole him away while we slept.

14 And if this come to the governor's ears, we will persuade him, and secure you.

15 So they took the money, and did as they were taught: and this saying is commonly reported among the Jews until this day.

16 Then the eleven disciples went away into Galilee, into a mountain where Jesus had appointed them.

17 And when they saw him, they worshipped him: but some doubted.

18 And Jesus came and spake unto them, saying, All power is given unto me in heaven and in earth.

[19] Go ye therefore, and teach all nations, baptizing them in the name of the Father, and of the Son, and of the Holy Ghost:

[20] Teaching them to observe all things whatsoever I have commanded you: and, lo, I am with you alway, even unto the end of the world. Amen. [Matthew 28:1-20]

Mark 16:1-20

[1] And when the sabbath was past, Mary Magdalene, and Mary the mother of James, and Salome, had bought sweet spices, that they might come and anoint him.

[2] And very early in the morning the first day of the week, they came unto the sepulchre at the rising of the sun.

[3] And they said among themselves, Who shall roll us away the stone from the door of the sepulchre?

[4] And when they looked, they saw that the stone was rolled away: for it was very great.

[5] And entering into the sepulchre, they saw a young man sitting on the right side, clothed in a long white garment; and they were affrighted.

[6] And he saith unto them, Be not affrighted: Ye seek Jesus of Nazareth, which was crucified: he is risen; he is not here: behold the place where they laid him.

⁷ But go your way, tell his disciples and Peter that he goeth before you into Galilee: there shall ye see him, as he said unto you.
⁸ And they went out quickly, and fled from the sepulchre; for they trembled and were amazed: neither said they any thing to any man; for they were afraid.
⁹ Now when Jesus was risen early the first day of the week, he appeared first to Mary Magdalene, out of whom he had cast seven devils.
¹⁰ And she went and told them that had been with him, as they mourned and wept.
¹¹ And they, when they had heard that he was alive, and had been seen of her, believed not.
¹² After that he appeared in another form unto two of them, as they walked, and went into the country.
¹³ And they went and told it unto the residue: neither believed they them.
¹⁴ Afterward he appeared unto the eleven as they sat at meat, and upbraided them with their unbelief and hardness of heart, because they believed not them which had seen him after he was risen.
¹⁵ And he said unto them, Go ye into all the world, and preach the gospel to every creature.
¹⁶ He that believeth and is baptized shall be saved; but he that believeth not shall be damned.

¹⁷ And these signs shall follow them that believe; In my name shall they cast out devils; they shall speak with new tongues;
¹⁸ They shall take up serpents; and if they drink any deadly thing, it shall not hurt them; they shall lay hands on the sick, and they shall recover.
¹⁹ So then after the Lord had spoken unto them, he was received up into heaven, and sat on the right hand of God.
²⁰ And they went forth, and preached every where, the Lord working with them, and confirming the word with signs following. Amen. [Mark 16:1-20]

Luke 23:50-56; 24:1-53

⁵⁰ And, behold, there was a man named Joseph, a counsellor; and he was a good man, and a just:
⁵¹ (The same had not consented to the counsel and deed of them;) he was of Arimathaea, a city of the Jews: who also himself waited for the kingdom of God.
⁵² This man went unto Pilate, and begged the body of Jesus.
⁵³ And he took it down, and wrapped it in linen, and laid it in a sepulchre that was hewn in stone, wherein never man before was laid.
⁵⁴ And that day was the preparation, and the sabbath drew on.

55 And the women also, which came with him from Galilee, followed after, and beheld the sepulchre, and how his body was laid.

56 And they returned, and prepared spices and ointments; and rested the sabbath day according to the commandment.

1 Now upon the first day of the week, very early in the morning, they came unto the sepulchre, bringing the spices which they had prepared, and certain others with them.

2 And they found the stone rolled away from the sepulchre.

3 And they entered in, and found not the body of the Lord Jesus.

4 And it came to pass, as they were much perplexed thereabout, behold, two men stood by them in shining garments:

5 And as they were afraid, and bowed down their faces to the earth, they said unto them, Why seek ye the living among the dead?

6 He is not here, but is risen: remember how he spake unto you when he was yet in Galilee,

7 Saying, The Son of man must be delivered into the hands of sinful men, and be crucified, and the third day rise again.

8 And they remembered his words,

⁹ And returned from the sepulchre, and told all these things unto the eleven, and to all the rest.

¹⁰ It was Mary Magdalene, and Joanna, and Mary the mother of James, and other women that were with them, which told these things unto the apostles.

¹¹ And their words seemed to them as idle tales, and they believed them not.

¹² Then arose Peter, and ran unto the sepulchre; and stooping down, he beheld the linen clothes laid by themselves, and departed, wondering in himself at that which was come to pass.

¹³ And, behold, two of them went that same day to a village called Emmaus, which was from Jerusalem about threescore furlongs.

¹⁴ And they talked together of all these things which had happened.

¹⁵ And it came to pass, that, while they communed together and reasoned, Jesus himself drew near, and went with them.

¹⁶ But their eyes were holden that they should not know him.

¹⁷ And he said unto them, What manner of communications are these that ye have one to another, as ye walk, and are sad?

¹⁸ And the one of them, whose name was Cleopas, answering said unto him, Art thou only a stranger in Jerusalem, and hast not known the things which are come to pass there in these days?

19 And he said unto them, What things? And they said unto him, Concerning Jesus of Nazareth, which was a prophet mighty in deed and word before God and all the people:

20 And how the chief priests and our rulers delivered him to be condemned to death, and have crucified him.

21 But we trusted that it had been he which should have redeemed Israel: and beside all this, to day is the third day since these things were done.

22 Yea, and certain women also of our company made us astonished, which were early at the sepulchre;

23 And when they found not his body, they came, saying, that they had also seen a vision of angels, which said that he was alive.

24 And certain of them which were with us went to the sepulchre, and found it even so as the women had said: but him they saw not.

25 Then he said unto them, O fools, and slow of heart to believe all that the prophets have spoken:

26 Ought not Christ to have suffered these things, and to enter into his glory?

27 And beginning at Moses and all the prophets, he expounded unto them in all the scriptures the things concerning himself.

²⁸ And they drew nigh unto the village, whither they went: and he made as though he would have gone further.

²⁹ But they constrained him, saying, Abide with us: for it is toward evening, and the day is far spent. And he went in to tarry with them.

³⁰ And it came to pass, as he sat at meat with them, he took bread, and blessed it, and brake, and gave to them.

³¹ And their eyes were opened, and they knew him; and he vanished out of their sight.

³² And they said one to another, Did not our heart burn within us, while he talked with us by the way, and while he opened to us the scriptures?

³³ And they rose up the same hour, and returned to Jerusalem, and found the eleven gathered together, and them that were with them,

³⁴ Saying, The Lord is risen indeed, and hath appeared to Simon.

³⁵ And they told what things were done in the way, and how he was known of them in breaking of bread.

³⁶ And as they thus spake, Jesus himself stood in the midst of them, and saith unto them, Peace be unto you.

³⁷ But they were terrified and affrighted, and supposed that they had seen a spirit.

³⁸ And he said unto them, Why are ye troubled? and why do thoughts arise in your hearts?

³⁹ Behold my hands and my feet, that it is I myself: handle me, and see; for a spirit hath not flesh and bones, as ye see me have.

⁴⁰ And when he had thus spoken, he shewed them his hands and his feet.

⁴¹ And while they yet believed not for joy, and wondered, he said unto them, Have ye here any meat?

⁴² And they gave him a piece of a broiled fish, and of an honeycomb.

⁴³ And he took it, and did eat before them.

⁴⁴ And he said unto them, These are the words which I spake unto you, while I was yet with you, that all things must be fulfilled, which were written in the law of Moses, and in the prophets, and in the psalms, concerning me.

⁴⁵ Then opened he their understanding, that they might understand the scriptures,

⁴⁶ And said unto them, Thus it is written, and thus it behoved Christ to suffer, and to rise from the dead the third day:

⁴⁷ And that repentance and remission of sins should be preached in his name among all nations, beginning at Jerusalem.

⁴⁸ And ye are witnesses of these things.

⁴⁹ And, behold, I send the promise of my Father upon you: but tarry ye in the city of Jerusalem, until ye be endued with power from on high.

⁵⁰ And he led them out as far as to Bethany, and he lifted up his hands, and blessed them.

⁵¹ And it came to pass, while he blessed them, he was parted from them, and carried up into heaven.

⁵² And they worshipped him, and returned to Jerusalem with great joy:

⁵³ And were continually in the temple, praising and blessing God. Amen.

[Luke 24:1-53]

John 20:1-31; 21:1-14

¹ The first day of the week cometh Mary Magdalene early, when it was yet dark, unto the sepulchre, and seeth the stone taken away from the sepulchre.

² Then she runneth, and cometh to Simon Peter, and to the other disciple, whom Jesus loved, and saith unto them, They have taken away the Lord out of the sepulchre, and we know not where they have laid him.

³ Peter therefore went forth, and that other disciple, and came to the sepulchre.

⁴ So they ran both together: and the other disciple did outrun Peter, and came first to the sepulchre.

5 And he stooping down, and looking in, saw the linen clothes lying; yet went he not in.

6 Then cometh Simon Peter following him, and went into the sepulchre, and seeth the linen clothes lie,

7 And the napkin, that was about his head, not lying with the linen clothes, but wrapped together in a place by itself.

8 Then went in also that other disciple, which came first to the sepulchre, and he saw, and believed.

9 For as yet they knew not the scripture, that he must rise again from the dead.

10 Then the disciples went away again unto their own home.

11 But Mary stood without at the sepulchre weeping: and as she wept, she stooped down, and looked into the sepulchre,

12 And seeth two angels in white sitting, the one at the head, and the other at the feet, where the body of Jesus had lain.

13 And they say unto her, Woman, why weepest thou? She saith unto them, Because they have taken away my Lord, and I know not where they have laid him.

14 And when she had thus said, she turned herself back, and saw Jesus standing, and knew not that it was Jesus.

15 Jesus saith unto her, Woman, why weepest thou? whom seekest thou? She, supposing him to be the gardener, saith

unto him, Sir, if thou have borne him hence, tell me where thou hast laid him, and I will take him away.

16 Jesus saith unto her, Mary. She turned herself, and saith unto him, Rabboni; which is to say, Master.

17 Jesus saith unto her, Touch me not; for I am not yet ascended to my Father: but go to my brethren, and say unto them, I ascend unto my Father, and your Father; and to my God, and your God.

18 Mary Magdalene came and told the disciples that she had seen the Lord, and that he had spoken these things unto her.

19 Then the same day at evening, being the first day of the week, when the doors were shut where the disciples were assembled for fear of the Jews, came Jesus and stood in the midst, and saith unto them, Peace be unto you.

20 And when he had so said, he shewed unto them his hands and his side. Then were the disciples glad, when they saw the Lord.

21 Then said Jesus to them again, Peace be unto you: as my Father hath sent me, even so send I you.

22 And when he had said this, he breathed on them, and saith unto them, Receive ye the Holy Ghost:

23 Whose soever sins ye remit, they are remitted unto them; and whose soever sins ye retain, they are retained.

24 But Thomas, one of the twelve, called Didymus, was not with them when Jesus came.

25 The other disciples therefore said unto him, We have seen the Lord. But he said unto them, Except I shall see in his hands the print of the nails, and put my finger into the print of the nails, and thrust my hand into his side, I will not believe.

26 And after eight days again his disciples were within, and Thomas with them: then came Jesus, the doors being shut, and stood in the midst, and said, Peace be unto you.

27 Then saith he to Thomas, Reach hither thy finger, and behold my hands; and reach hither thy hand, and thrust it into my side: and be not faithless, but believing.

28 And Thomas answered and said unto him, My Lord and my God.

29 Jesus saith unto him, Thomas, because thou hast seen me, thou hast believed: blessed are they that have not seen, and yet have believed.

30 And many other signs truly did Jesus in the presence of his disciples, which are not written in this book:

31 But these are written, that ye might believe that Jesus is the Christ, the Son of

God; and that believing ye might have life through his name.

¹ After these things Jesus shewed himself again to the disciples at the sea of Tiberias; and on this wise shewed he himself.

² There were together Simon Peter, and Thomas called Didymus, and Nathanael of Cana in Galilee, and the sons of Zebedee, and two other of his disciples.

³ Simon Peter saith unto them, I go a fishing. They say unto him, We also go with thee. They went forth, and entered into a ship immediately; and that night they caught nothing.

⁴ But when the morning was now come, Jesus stood on the shore: but the disciples knew not that it was Jesus.

⁵ Then Jesus saith unto them, Children, have ye any meat? They answered him, No.

⁶ And he said unto them, Cast the net on the right side of the ship, and ye shall find. They cast therefore, and now they were not able to draw it for the multitude of fishes.

⁷ Therefore that disciple whom Jesus loved saith unto Peter, It is the Lord. Now when Simon Peter heard that it was the Lord, he girt his fisher's coat unto him, (for he was naked,) and did cast himself into the sea.

⁸ And the other disciples came in a little ship; (for they were not far from land, but as it were two hundred cubits,) dragging the net with fishes.

⁹ As soon then as they were come to land, they saw a fire of coals there, and fish laid thereon, and bread.

¹⁰ Jesus saith unto them, Bring of the fish which ye have now caught.

¹¹ Simon Peter went up, and drew the net to land full of great fishes, an hundred and fifty and three: and for all there were so many, yet was not the net broken.

¹² Jesus saith unto them, Come and dine. And none of the disciples durst ask him, Who art thou? knowing that it was the Lord.

¹³ Jesus then cometh, and taketh bread, and giveth them, and fish likewise.

¹⁴ This is now the third time that Jesus shewed himself to his disciples, after that he was risen from the dead.

[John 20:1-31; 21:1-14]

Three Common Topics In Each Gospel Narrative

Next, I want to show **three common topics** or themes that I see in each Gospel narrative:

1) Women go to the sepulchre (tomb) of Jesus
2) Men, angels and/or Jesus appear to the women
3) Jesus appears to the disciples

1) <u>Women go to the sepulchre (tomb) of Jesus</u>

Matthew: Mary Magdalene and the other Mary
Mark: Mary Magdalene, Mary the mother of James and Salome.
Luke: Mary Magdalene, Joanna and Mary the mother of James and other women (unnamed).
John: Mary Magdalene by herself.

2) <u>Men, angels and/or Jesus appear to the women</u>

Matthew: An angel appears to the women after rolling away the stone. Then, Jesus appears to the women on their way to see the disciples.
Mark: A young man is found sitting on the right side. When Jesus was risen early the first day of the week, he appeared first to Mary Magdalene.
Luke: Two men appear in shining garments.
John: After returning for a second time, Mary Magdalene sees two angels in white. Turning back, she sees Jesus who she assumes is the gardener. After Jesus makes himself known to her, Mary goes to tell the remaining disciples.

3) <u>Jesus appears to the disciples</u>

Matthew: The remaining eleven disciples went to Galilee, into a mountain previously shown them, and Jesus appears to them.
Mark: Jesus first appears to two men, then he appears to the eleven as they eat a meal (in Jerusalem).
Luke: Two men, on the road to Emmaus, walk with Jesus. Afterwards, the two run to Jerusalem where the eleven are gathered. Jesus shows up, and then asks for something to eat. Jesus leads

them all to Bethany where he ascends to heaven. The disciples return to Jerusalem and worship at the temple.

John: Jesus appears to the disciples in the evening (in Jerusalem). He breathes 'the Holy Ghost' upon them. After these things, Jesus showed himself 'at the sea of Tiberias.' (the sea of Galilee). Jesus eats there with them thereafter.

Is The Inconsistent Telling Of The Same Incident — A Telltale Sign Of Lying?

In modern day Police investigations it is a common practice to ask an accused person to repeat their stories multiple times. A telltale sign that someone is lying is that the stories change in some aspect each time they are told.

By looking at the topical comparison, above, I believe it is quite clear that for the event which is purported to be **the most attested in all of human history, those writing the accounts could not quite get their stories straight!**

What About The Resurrection (And Ascension)?

So, if you were to ask me if I thought that Jesus rose from the dead, I would have to answer, **"When the purported eye witnesses could not seem to get their stories straight, how should it be that I could say that I believe, beyond a shadow of a doubt, that Jesus rose from the dead and ascended?"**

Jesus Cannot Be The Jewish Messiah*

71

*If He Ever Took The Authoritative Hebrew-Language Based Jewish Scriptures Out Of Their Plain And Natural Context, Misquoted, Misrepresented, Misappropriated, Contravened Them Or Otherwise Treated Them With Contempt And Disrespect!

I realize that statement is a long sentence! **Essentially, it is my belief that Jesus cannot be the Jewish Messiah if he actually misquoted the Holy Prophets of יְהֹוָה [Yehovah]!**

---

71 Ratchel Claire, 'Cute lamb standing in enclosure in countryside,' accessed 8 May 2023, https://www.pexels.com/photo/cute-lamb-standing-in-enclosure-in-countryside-5490714/. Converted to grayscale and cropped.

You may have surmised that I believe in the authority of the Hebrew-language based Jewish Scriptures, sourced from the ancient Leningrad Codex.

The prophet, Daniel, gave a timeline to the coming of a Messiah, an anointed one.[72] Based upon that timeline, no other well-known figure in human history comes close to fulfilling the role of a Messiah other than Jesus of Nazareth (יֵשׁוּעַ – the Hebrew name; and the transliterated Hebrew name, 'Yeshua')!

I also believe that The Messiah's essential messaging was stolen and obfuscated by none other than Saul of Tarsus, aka the false prophet and self-appointed Apostle Paul!

His influence plagues prophetic understanding to this very day.

Moreover, I believe that essential messaging of the Messiah has been promulgated through popular books, like **'The Great Late Planet Earth.'**[73] That book was a huge influence on American society after its release in 1970.[74]

The 'premillennial' viewpoint employs a creative dating system requiring the breaking of Daniel's timeline into a **'part back**

---

[72] Daniel 9:24-27:

[24] Seventy weeks are decreed upon thy people and upon thy holy city, to finish the transgression, and to make an end of sin, and to forgive iniquity, and to bring in everlasting righteousness, and to seal vision and prophet, and to anoint the most holy place.

[25] Know therefore and discern, that from the going forth of the word to restore and to build Yerushalam unto Mashiach, the conspicuous leader, shall be seven weeks; and for sixty-two weeks, it shall be built again, with broad place and moat, but in troublous times.

[26] And after the sixty-two weeks shall Mashiach be cut off, and be no more; and the people of the ruler that shall come shall destroy the city and the sanctuary; but his end shall be with a flood; and unto the end of the war desolations are determined.

[27] And he shall make a firm covenant with many for one week; and for half of the week he shall cause the sacrifice and the offering to cease; and upon the wing of detestable things shall be that which causeth appalment; and that until the extermination wholly determined be poured out upon that which causeth appalment.'

[73] Hal Lindsey with C.C. Carlson, "The Late Great Planet Earth," (Grand Rapids, MI, Zondervan).

[74] My own atheist mother bought the book around that time. After she read it, she asked me and my brother to read it. Thus, we also became familiar with the Christian 'premillennial' prophetic belief system espoused in that book!

then' and a 'part sometime in the future thousands of years removed.' Their presumption for a late date for fulfillment appears to have **forced** this creativity, taking the original passage, from Daniel 9, and obfuscating it's plain meaning!

The modern **'Christian premillennial prophetic belief system'** is bantered about throughout the book, 'The Late Great Planet Earth.' Interestingly, <u>that</u> <u>premillennial</u> <u>viewpoint</u> **<u>depends</u> <u>upon</u> <u>a</u> <u>late</u> <u>dating</u> <u>of</u> <u>the</u> <u>book</u> <u>of</u> <u>Revelation</u>.**

If the the book of Revelation could be shown to have **been written prior to the destruction of the Temple** in Jerusalem in 70 A.D., then the stories of the horrors of those Israelites imprisoned within its walls by the Roman army, such as mothers eating their own children due to starvation, may have been shown to be possible evidence for fulfillment of events found in the prophetic language of its writings!

Suffice it to say, as in so many other Christian writings, I believe there are a plethora of out-of-context quotations from the Jewish Scriptures used for internal validation in 'The Late Great Planet Earth,' which are just too numerous to explore herein.

Regarding Christian exegesis, taking even their own New Testament books out of their natural contexts appears to be a common practice among modern Christians in their dissection of texts to promote their particular viewpoints.

Quite interesting, Chapter 2 of the book of Revelation appears to be a direct warning regarding the self-appointed Apostle Paul, **'and thou hast tried them which say they are apostles, and are not, and hast found them liars'** [Rev. 2:2b]:

> 2 I know thy works, and thy labour, and thy patience, and how thou canst not bear them which are evil: and thou hast tried them which say they are apostles, and are not, and hast found them liars:

3 And hast borne, and hast patience, and for my name's sake hast laboured, and hast not fainted. [Revelation 2:2-3]

I am of the opinion that the Revelation 2 passage could be why there probably was a _hostile_ _polemic_ _between_ _Luke_ _and_ _the_ _Apostle_ _John_.

The reader may not be aware of this, **as it is subtle.** Also, modern day views of the 1st century are clouded by a substantial Roman Catholic, 'Christian,' history of the time.

Revelation 2:2 clearly speaks about **'trying those who say they are apostles but are not, and hast found them liars.'** To the actual historical first century, mostly lost to us, I believe it was likely well known in Jewish oriented circles that Paul was a self-proclaimed, self-appointed Apostle, **as warned by Jesus in Matthew 24!**

How could this be, you might ask?

The answer, to me, lies somewhere **'in-between-the-lines.'** Notably, the only place that has John ('the disciple, whom Jesus loved') and Peter run together to the tomb where Jesus was buried is found in the Gospel of John. That incident is found nowhere else! Yet, if you ask any Christian, almost every one would say, matter-of-factly, that John ran to the tomb with Peter.

Having boasted that he had basically exhausted all eye-witness sources for information, Luke, in the preamble to the book of Luke and to that in Acts, writing to a Theophilus, expressed a thorough research. However, regarding the narrative of the story of going to Jesus's tomb, Luke identified only Peter as having gone there by himself. He doesn't mention John at all![75]

---

75 John Paul Adams, 'The Tomb of Jesus on Easter Morning,' last modified 20 Apr 2014, http://www.csun.edu/~hcfll004/Easter-Tomb.html.

I think Revelation 2:2 shows John's wariness for false apostle Paul! That is my **'in-between-the-lines view'** of why friend-of-Paul—Luke didn't mention John with Peter going to the tomb.

Luke boldly appears to claim that he was extremely meticulous in researching events about Jesus. Yet, for him apparently not to have used John as a source, nor mention him as to have gone to the tomb with Peter, **seems disingenuous to me!**

Returning to a central Messiah figure, I approach the subject by first asking, *"What would the nature and the purpose of any messenger of the Almighty be, including 'The Messiah'?"*

Within my own biases I would answer, *"The purpose of any messenger of Almighty God would be to give Yehovah glory and reflect the essence of His divine nature by trying to serve Him wholeheartedly, following all of His commandments and statutes found in the written Torah, and encouraging others to do the same!"*

Thus, my reasoning is somewhat based upon my belief of just what *'the Messiah'* was to be about in the first place, notwithstanding the person, Jesus, and what has been written and assumed about him over the last two thousand years!

In the least, I believe that **any Messiah type figure would be a prophet** or like a prophet. There is a defining passage in the book of Deuteronomy which indicates that **a prophet to come would be like Moses:**

> **¹³ Thou shalt be whole-hearted with Yehovah thy God.**
> **¹⁴ For these nations, that thou art to dispossess, hearken unto soothsayers, and unto diviners; but as for thee, Yehovah thy God hath not suffered thee so to do.**

¹⁵ A prophet will Yehovah thy God raise up unto thee, from the midst of thee, of thy brethren, like unto me; unto him ye shall hearken;

¹⁶ according to all that thou didst desire of Yehovah thy God in Horeb in the day of the assembly, saying: 'Let me not hear again the voice of Yehovah my God, neither let me see this great fire any more, that I die not.'

¹⁷ And Yehovah said unto me: 'They have well said that which they have spoken.

¹⁸ I will raise them up a prophet from among their brethren, like unto thee; and I will put My words in his mouth, and he shall speak unto them all that I shall command him.

¹⁹ And it shall come to pass, that whosoever will not hearken unto My words which he shall speak in My name, I will require it of him.

²⁰ But the prophet, that shall speak a word presumptuously in My name, which I have not commanded him to speak, or that shall speak in the name of other gods, that same prophet shall die.'

²¹ And if thou say in thy heart: 'How shall we know the word which Yehovah hath not spoken?'

22 When a prophet speaketh in the name of Yehovah, if the thing follow not, nor come to pass, that is the thing which Yehovah hath not spoken; the prophet hath spoken it presumptuously, thou shalt not be afraid of him.
[Deuteronomy 18:13-22]

From the context of part of that discourse being directed to the people of Israel, "**... according to all that thou didst desire of Yehovah thy God in Horeb in the day of the assembly, ...**", the prophet to come could easily be said to be **Joshua**, who followed Moses as leader of the Israelite people.

No doubt but as Moses aged, the Israelite people probably had concerns about what direction the nation would take after his death. That could have easily brought about the reason to have the above passage rendered, so that an expectation of a continuous revelation in its leaders would ensue.

I am aware, however, that rather than looking to the Jewish Scriptures as a way to show the one who was to follow Moses, many Christian apologists believe that the above passage in Deuteronomy 18 is **referring to Jesus, rather than to Joshua!** No doubt, but **Luke is the likely source for that belief!**

22 For Moses truly said unto the fathers, A prophet shall the Lord your God raise up unto you of your brethren, like unto me; him shall ye hear in all things whatsoever he shall say unto you.
23 And it shall come to pass, that every soul, which will not hear that prophet, shall be destroyed from among the people.
24 Yea, and all the prophets from Samuel and those that follow after, as many as have spoken, have likewise foretold of these days.
[Acts 3:22-24]

[37] This is that Moses, which said unto the children of Israel, A prophet shall the Lord your God raise up unto you of your brethren, like unto me; him shall ye hear. [Acts 7:37]

Yet, in Numbers, there is a passage which clearly shows that which is prophesied in Deuteronomy 18 as being fulfilled:

15 And Moses spoke unto Yehovah, saying:

16 'Let Yehovah, the God of the spirits of all flesh, set a man over the congregation,

17 who may go out before them, and who may come in before them, and who may lead them out, and who may bring them in; that the congregation of Yehovah be not as sheep which have no shepherd.'

18 And Yehovah said unto Moses: 'Take thee Joshua the son of Nun, a man in whom is spirit, and lay thy hand upon him;

19 and set him before Eleazar the priest, and before all the congregation; and give him a charge in their sight.

20 And thou shalt put of thy honour upon him, that all the congregation of the children of Israel may hearken.

21 And he shall stand before Eleazar the priest, who shall inquire for him by the judgment of the Urim before Yehovah; at his word shall they go out, and at his word they shall come in, both

he, and all the children of Israel with him, even all the congregation.'
[Numbers 27:15-21]

I find it unfortunate and disconcerting that Christian teachers **(as well as Luke, in Acts)** have fomented a pattern of thought that the entire Jewish Scriptures are full of *Messianic predictions and allusions,* **and more particularly that Jesus is the intended protagonist throughout its pages!**

A cogent example can be found in a well known story from the book of Daniel, when 'Shadrach, Meshach and Abed-Nego'[76] are thrown into 'the fiery furnace' by Nebuchadnezzar, and they are joined by a *fourth being* in their midst. Many Christians will express that they *absolutely know* that the fourth being is none other than Jesus! Others claim it to be the archangel Michael.

Otherwise, any time there is a mention of "God," many of them insert into their own minds that it is *"Jesus"* instead, simply because they have incorporated the **teachings of Paul to believe that the man Jesus is Almighty God in the flesh!**

That is a presupposition of the text being something other than its plain and simple meaning, *and trying to prove a present belief system from a different context in the past.*

To me, this is a nutty doctrine, similar in a sense to the Catholic belief of *transubstantiation,*[77] whereby they believe that the elements of their 'Eucharist' are *magically* turned into real flesh and blood of the man Jesus, presumably in his physical state before crucifixion, expressed in *his words at the Lord's Supper, aka the last supper.*[78]

---

[76] Book of Daniel, Chapter 3.
[77] Cal Christiansen, 'How can I explain transubstantiation?,' Northwest Catholic, last updated 29 Sep 2016, https://nwcatholic.org/voices/cal-christiansen/how-can-i-explain-transubstantiation.
[78] The Lord's Supper passages are found in Matt 26:26-29, Mark 14:22-25, Luke 22:19-20. Note, that it is also referred to as 'The Last Supper.'

In this present case, when Christians substitute the name, Jesus, for others within the text of the Jewish Scriptures, they force a construction of meaning clearly outside of the intent of the immediate context in the source.

I would like to return to the idea of 'a prophet like unto Moses,' if only to describe Moses. **Moses was humble.** He led the children of Israel out of Egypt. He is attributed to having written the entire five books of the Torah. When reading the Torah, very seldom is one aware of its authorship. Moses was a natural-born storyteller, giving rich narratives for us to dwell upon.

A True Prophet Would Never Contravene The Torah!

I believe any discussion regarding the Messiah would have to be centered around an understanding that a **true prophet of Yehovah would never contravene the teachings found in the Jewish Scriptures and more particularly, the Torah!**

It is my opinion **that understanding should be applied to Jesus of Nazareth as well.**

Thus, any time there is a narrative found in the New Testament which expresses that Jesus does something contrary to the

---

Matthew 26:26-28

26 And as they were eating, Jesus took bread, and blessed it, and brake it, and gave it to the disciples, and said, Take, eat; this is my body.

27 And he took the cup, and gave thanks, and gave it to them, saying, Drink ye all of it;

28 For this is my blood of the new testament, which is shed for many for the remission of sins.
Mark 14:22-24

22 And as they did eat, Jesus took bread, and blessed, and brake it, and gave to them, and said, Take, eat: this is my body.

23 And he took the cup, and when he had given thanks, he gave it to them: and they all drank of it.

24 And he said unto them, This is my blood of the new testament, which is shed for many.
Luke 22:19-20

19 And he took bread, and gave thanks, and brake it, and gave unto them, saying, This is my body which is given for you: this do in remembrance of me.

20 Likewise also the cup after supper, saying, This cup is the new testament in my blood, which is shed for you.

clear teachings of the Torah, I do not entertain that story to actually be from or about **the Messiah,** who would, in the least in the core of his essence, also be a prophet of the Almighty!

Casting Out The Money-Changers

12 And Jesus went into the temple of God, and cast out all them that sold and bought in the temple, and overthrew the tables of the moneychangers, and the seats of them that sold doves,
13 And said unto them, It is written, My house shall be called the house of prayer; but ye have made it a den of thieves. [Matthew 21:12-13]

15 And they come to Jerusalem: and Jesus went into the temple, and began to cast out them that sold and bought in the temple, and overthrew the tables of the moneychangers, and the seats of them that sold doves;
16 And would not suffer that any man should carry any vessel through the temple.
17 And he taught, saying unto them, Is it not written, My house shall be called of all nations the house of prayer? but ye have made it a den of thieves. [Mark 11:15-17]

45 And he went into the temple, and began to cast out them that sold therein, and them that bought;

46 Saying unto them, It is written, My house is the house of prayer: but ye have made it a den of thieves. [Luke 19:45-46]

Those same passages, are presented side-by-side in the following:

"House of Prayer" — "Den of Thieves" In The Synoptic Gospels (KJV)

Matthew 21:12-13	Mark 11:15-17	Luke 19:45-46
12 And Jesus went into the temple of God, and cast out all them that sold and bought in the temple, and over-threw the tables of the moneychangers, and the seats of them that sold doves, 13 And said unto them, It is written My house shall be called the house of prayer; but ye have made it a den of thieves.	15 And they come to Jerusalem: and Jesus went into the temple and began to cast out them that sold and bought in the temple, and overthrew the tables of the montychangers, and the seats of them that sold doves. 16 And would not suffer that any man should carry any vessel through the temple. 17 And he taught, saying unto them, Is it not written, My house shall be called of all nations the house of prayer? but ye have made it a den of thieves.	45 And he went into the temple, and began to cast out them that sold therein, and them that bought; 46 Saying unto them, It is written, My house is the house of prayer: but ye have made it a den of thieves.

"House of Prayer" In Isaiah 56:6-8

כִּי בֵיתִי בֵּית־תְּפִלָּה יִקָּרֵא לְכָל־הָעַמִּים

My House Shall Be Called
A House Of Prayer For All Peoples

6 Also the aliens, that join themselves to Yehovah, to minister unto Him, and to love the name of Yehovah, to be His servants, every one that keepeth the sabbath from profaning it, and holdeth fast by My covenant:
7 Even them will I bring to My holy mountain, and make them joyful in My house of prayer; their burnt-offerings and their sacrifices shall be acceptable upon Mine altar; for My house shall be called a house of prayer for all peoples.
8 Saith the Lord GOD [Adonai Yehovi] who gathereth the dispersed of Israel: Yet I will gather others to him, beside those of him that are gathered. [Is. 56:6-8]

The Isaiah 56 passage refers to Gentiles (aliens)! It clearly expresses **that they are included** with the children of Israel _ONLY IF THEY KEEP THE SAME COMMANDMENTS, INCLUDING OBSERVING THE SEVENTH-DAY SABBATHS._ Verse 7 also shows that their '**burnt-offerings and sacrifices** shall be acceptable upon Mine altar.'

Each of the New Testament quotations for "My House Shall Be Called A House Of Prayer For All Peoples" — are actually _misquotations_, misrepresentations of the context in Isaiah!

Isaiah is concerned with obedience to the commandments as found in the Torah, and says absolutely nothing about making the House of Yehovah a 'Den of robbers' as is in **Jeremiah 7:**

"Den of Robbers" In Jeremiah 7

הַמְעָרַת פָּרִצִים הָיָה הַבַּיִת הַזֶּה אֲשֶׁר־נִקְרָא־שְׁמִי

עָלָיו בְּעֵינֵיכֶם גַּם אָנֹכִי הִנֵּה רָאִיתִי נְאֻם־יְהוָה׃

Is This House ... Become A Den of Robbers...?

9 **Will ye steal, murder, and commit adultery, and swear falsely, and offer unto Baal, and walk after other gods whom ye have not known,**

10 **and come and stand before Me in this house, whereupon My name is called, and say: 'We are delivered', that ye may do all these abominations?**

11 **Is this house, whereupon My name is called, become a den of robbers in your eyes? Behold, I, even I, have seen it, saith Yehovah.**

12 **For go ye now unto My place which was in Shiloh, where I caused My name to dwell at the first, and see what I did to it for the wickedness of My people Israel.**

13 **And now, because ye have done all these works, saith Yehovah, and I spoke unto you, speaking betimes and often, but ye heard not, and I called you, but ye answered not;**

¹⁴ therefore will I do unto the house, whereupon My name is called, wherein ye trust, and unto the place which I gave to you and to your fathers, as I have done to Shiloh. [Jeremiah 7:9-14]

As in Isaiah, the Jeremiah 7 passage shows a completely different context than that which is quoted, portrayed and even inferred in the Synoptic Gospel accounts!

In an attempt to be fair, however, the Jeremiah 7:9 passage **does express a rebuke,** "Will ye steal, murder, and commit adultery, and swear falsely, and offer unto Baal, and walk after the other gods whom ye have not known."

I think just a mere mention of Jesus casting out money-changers and those who sold doves, etc. *would have been sufficient* in representing the incident (showing a rebuke) in the original text.

However, It appears to me to be that the authors/scribes were more interested in **showing that Jesus somehow was fulfilling prophecy for the Messiah** so they would have put the embellishments about the house of prayer and den of thieves as their way of expressing a prophetic fulfillment.

The Jeremiah 7:11 verse asks, in context, 'Is this house ... become a den of robbers in your eyes?' — *NOT, __but you have MADE it a den of robbers__* — as the Synoptic Gospel quotations would lead you to believe!

The context of Jeremiah 7 is clearly about how Israel had forsaken יְהֹוָה [Yehovah], committing abominations, and forsaking Him; and he basically tells them He will destroy His House just like He did when it was in Shiloh.

None of the referenced New Testament passages have anything to say about **Gentiles <u>being joined to Israel</u>,** nor to do so that they would have to keep the Sabbaths and the rest of the commandments — just as Israelite Jews are so obligated. **That is, indeed, the actual context of the quoted passage in Isaiah!**

Again, even the Jeremiah 7:11 passage is misquoted as **all three references speak of '<u>You</u>' <u>making the House of Yehovah a</u> '<u>den of robbers</u>.**' That Jeremiah passage clearly shows that the reference to robbers, in context, is with a greater question essentially emphasizing that **the <u>audience sees the House of Yehovah as a den of robbers,</u> <u>*not that they have made it so*</u>.**

I realize that **this is a subtle difference,** but because it makes it **appear that Jesus is fulfilling prophecy** as given in the Jewish Scriptures, **its inclusion is quite deceptive.**

Taking these things into consideration, I believe that the "It is written" passages from Matthew, Mark and Luke would most likely **not have been part of any original narrative** given by a native Israelite Jew familiar with the Jewish Scriptures.

Even more so, to believe that *their* Holy One of Israel, The King Messiah – Jesus – **would ever misquote or misrepresent the Holy Scriptures,** is to discredit even the idea of a chief Messiah, let alone to denigrate the person of Jesus with such impunity — which, in my opinion, is exactly what has been done in these passages in the Christian Bible!

At best, the references to the passages in Isaiah and Jeremiah make their inclusion ***poetic, not prophetic!*** However, a discerning individual should easily see that the referenced passages blatantly misrepresent the original Hebrew-language based Jewish texts. Neither the Isaiah nor the Jeremiah passages are prophetic in nature and there is absolutely no inference therein regarding the Messiah.

Jesus Cannot Be The Messiah ...
IF HE ACTUALLY *MISQUOTED*
THE HOLY PROPHETS OF יְהֹוָה [Yehovah]!

– The Christian Conundrum: To Insist That Jesus Absolutely Made These Statements Essentially *Condemns Him For Misquoting The Words of Yehovah As Given By His Holy Prophets!*

A true Prophet of יְהֹוָה [Yehovah] would *never* misquote the **Holy Scriptures** and take them so out of their original contexts!

Each of these New Testament passages begins with a similar phrase, "It Is Written" or "Is It Not Written". No doubt, but these passages refer to the "Jewish Scriptures" as to where the "It is written" phrases point to.

Yet, what most "Christians" do when "quoting from that event" is to *meld* all three New Testament quotes together, coming up with what is closer to the Mark 11:17 quotation:

> "'And he taught, saying unto them, Is it not written,
> My house shall be called of all nations the house
> of prayer? but you have made it a den of thieves."

Again, there is actually no single passage in all of the Jewish Scriptures where that, or a similarly *melded* phrase, is written or inferred. Rather, **it is a compilation** from Isaiah 56:7 and Jeremiah 7:11 — two separate passages by two separate authors, neither of which is a prophecy about the Messiah!

Why Would I Labor To Continue To Emphasize This?

What can this mean? **Is there a possibility that Jesus is actually quoted accurately** in all three Synoptic Gospels? If so, **he obviously didn't understand** the context of the original passages or was unaware (like modern Christians) that He was *melding* the Isaiah and Jeremiah passages into one phrase.

Or, does it mean that Jesus actually ***did NOT say these things*** as quoted, and that the original authors or later scribes who may have inserted these stories did so without having a thorough understanding of the original contexts in the Jewish Scriptures?

I lean towards the latter scenario!

I believe that Jesus is the promised Mashiach (Messiah), based upon the **timeline prophecy from Daniel 9.** However, I believe that the Messiah would be a true prophet of the Almighty God.

I absolutely do not believe that any bona fide prophet, and more so, an anointed – Messiah, would have come with the purpose of creating a completely **new religion disassociated from its supposed source** as found in the Jewish Scripture, removing the requirement of circumcision for all males, removing all laws for food consumption including what Yehovah considers to be *abominations.* **Dishonoring the written Torah** should not be a prerequisite for one to be considered as Messiah, IMHO!

However, that does not mean that I embrace the Christian idea of the Messiah, nor the teachings of Paul, especially when they circumvent, contravene and misappropriate the words of the Torah! I view Christianity to essentially being the initial creation of Paul, who established his doctrines based upon lying, *demonic familiar spirit friends* **in private encounters!**

Why do I hold the view that the original authors or later scribes **failed** in their attempt to accurately reference the oft-quoted "House of Prayer For All Peoples?"

Simply to illustrate the arrogance of "Pauline Christian" interpretation, which often does a great injustice to the original context of the referenced passages in the Jewish Scriptures.

Moreover, the New Testament not only takes the original passages out of context but somehow also makes it appear that in quoting them they are **authenticating Jesus as *fulfilling prophecy*** for the Jewish Messiah, when the references are clearly not intended to be prophetic in that way at all!

In my opinion, to attribute those words to Jesus **_would_ _absolutely_ _disqualify_ _him_ _as_ _a_ _candidate_ _of_ _being_ _the_ _Messiah_** — plain and simple.

Thus, you may see that I do not consider the Christian New Testament as authoritative Scripture — treating it the same as The Word of God found in the Hebrew-language based Jewish Scriptures! To me, that idea is simply a grand delusion.

In my opinion, to consider the New Testament as bona fide Scripture would be to diminish the majesty of Yehovah just as it is actually denigratory to the man, Jesus. This is because it especially attributes to him so many misquotations and out-of-context interpretations of the original Hebrew-language based Jewish Scriptures! **IMHO**, using a late dated, spurious Greek Septuagint to authenticate Biblical references is to blatantly mischaracterize the Torah.

In the same way that Saul of Tarsus was a False Prophet because he gave at least one prophecy for an event when there is absolutely no **incontrovertible evidence** that it ever occurred, I must emphasize that Jesus of Nazareth cannot be considered to be **"the Jewish Messiah"** if he ever misquoted the authoritative Jewish Scriptures, took them out of their natural contexts or misrepresented them in any way!

In summary, I do not know of any individual who might be considered to be the one that would come to Israel at and around the time of what we now consider to be the first century other than Jesus of Nazareth (see timeline in Daniel 9:24-27).

But what do I think that Jesus, as Messiah, might accomplish?

I think it is quite clear from what we can glean from New Testament authors after ***disengaging*** from the writings of Paul and Luke, among others under their influence, **that Jesus was directly opposed to the Pharisaic rabbinic authorities of his day**[79] and was concerned with showing that adherence to the teachings of the written Torah was paramount in understanding the will of Yehovah!

Then, what is your view about following the Messiah?

I understand that most non-Jews have the New Testament model in mind when thinking about the person of the Messiah. Otherwise, most Jews hold to the idea of the Messiah based upon the writings of Rashi and Maimonides.

I believe that the Messiah would come to reinforce the plain meaning and context of the written Jewish Scriptures to glorify Almighty God. I also believe that the Messiah would be opposed to any teachings of man such as the rabbinic authorities of his day, primarily because they opposed the authority of the written Jewish Scriptures and yet promoted their own discourses above the actual words of the prophets of Almighty God!

Any idea of the Messiah initiating the creation of a separate religious system founded upon the teachings of a false prophet, and self-corroborated from the ***spurious*** Greek Septuagint, is absolutely ludicrous to me.

Also, nullifying the plain and simple instructions found in the Hebrew-language based Jewish Scriptures and even opposing their directives is a totally foreign concept for any prophet of Yehovah, or for one to be considered as 'The Jewish Messiah!'

---

[79] Matthew 23 is a good example.

In my opinion, to follow the direct teachings of the written Torah, faithfully eschewing the unscriptural teachings of rabbinic, self-appointed, authorities as well as those promulgated by the self-appointed Apostle Paul, is following the essential message of the Messiah!

If that view interferes with or contravenes your own concepts and beliefs, I do not apologize for mine!

But you haven't mentioned what the Orthodox Jewish (Talmudic) community actually expects for a Messiah!

Of course, I might also be remiss if I failed to provide some information regarding **'Moshiach'** from the more orthodox Jewish community.

I mentioned earlier how that the writings of Maimonides and Rashi appear to me to be some of the earliest Jewish writings regarding the Messiah. I believe the ideas, for the most part, within Judaism as a whole regarding Moshiach all came upon the historical scene to shape current Messianic views after the time of those men.

Regardless, for the concept of The Messiah, I list below some of the better known ideas from a more orthodox Jewish standpoint:[80]

- **He would be a descendant of King David and King Solomon**
- **He would be wiser than Solomon**
- **He would be a prophet like Moses**

---

[80] A simple internet search using the term Moshiach will reveal these things. Some of the sites pulled up to provide the list are:
https://www.chabad.org/library/article_cdo/aid/1121893/jewish/Who-Is-Moshiach-the-Jewish-Messiah.htm,
https://www.ohrtmimim.org/Moshiach,
https://www.chabad.org/library/article_cdo/aid/332562/jewish/Moshiach-101.htm.

- **He would rule the world**
- **He would uphold the 613 commandments for Jews and the seven Noahide laws for Gentiles**
- **He would be an expert in Oral Torah**
- **He will rebuild the Holy Temple**

It may be noted that these bulleted items for the concept of the Jewish Moshiach follow Talmudic, rabbinic expectations.

In my opinion, modern rabbis have little desire to hold the written Torah as authoritative. Rather, they place authority in the rabbinic writings found in the Talmud, the oral tradition.

I have said elsewhere that I believe that the rabbis consider themselves, collectively, to actually be Elohim – God! In the least, they certainly act like it, demanding that their own edicts (תַּקָּנוֹת takkanot) be followed as divinely inspired law.

On the other hand, my own expectations for **'Mashiach'** follow my own biases regarding holding the written Hebrew-language based Jewish Scriptures as the ultimate authority.

My own list might look something like the following for the manner of Messiah:

- **He would love יְהֹוָה Yehovah with all of his heart**
- **Like King David, he would be a Jewish man after God's own heart; he would be anointed by Yehovah**
- **He would uphold the written Jewish Scriptures as authoritative, keep the commandments and statutes written therein, and teach others to do the same**
- **He would forsake all the teachings which oppose the written Torah, and he would especially be opposed to the so-called Oral Tradition and also the influence of its codification in the later, written Talmud.**

Similarly, his followers would have watched for deceivers; they would have recognized, as such, the False Prophet, the self-appointed Apostle Paul

- **He would welcome Gentiles into the nation of Israel who honor and keep the commandments and statutes written in the Torah, and whose males are circumcised. He would acknowledge the Jewish Scriptures for teachings regarding Gentiles[81]**
- **He would not even consider creating a new religion**
- **He would hate evil and love the truth**

I mentioned, previously, that, based upon the timeline given by the prophet Daniel, I believed that Jesus of Nazareth is that person, that Messiah figure. From what I can glean from the information available, **he fulfilled the above in my own list!**

As such, I do not look to a <u>future</u> 'coming of a Messiah.'

We still have the written Torah, which has been graciously passed down to us by those known as Masoretes, in the Leningrad Codex (It is the oldest, complete rendering of the Jewish Scriptures in existence. It was written in Egypt and is dated around the year 1008-1009 C.E. It is called the Leningrad Codex, because it is housed in a museum in St. Petersburg, Russia, formerly called Leningrad).

Moreover, I do not believe that there is a progression of prophetic Scriptural passages leading to a Messianic figure who would meet a self-defined criteria for leadership, and then create an entirely ***new religion*** having little to do with the actual Jewish Scriptures or that would blatantly disregard them.

---

[81] For example (Exodus 12:48-49):

48 And when a stranger shall sojourn with thee, and will keep the passover to Yehovah, let all his males be circumcised, and then let him come near and keep it; and he shall be as one that is born in the land; but no uncircumcised person shall eat thereof. 49 One Torah shall be to him that is homeborn, and unto the stranger that sojourneth among you.'

It might also be said that the religion created and maintained by the Jewish Talmudic rabbis *is **also** **a** **new** **religion** in and of itself! Modern Judaism is primarily based upon the teachings of the Oral Tradition, the Oral Torah — **rabbinic fiction**, IMHO! Please note that I do not oppose everything in the Talmud, but I would never want to view it as the direct word of Yehovah!

Obviously, the Christian model asserts that Jesus will return and conquer all opposition and then rule in Jerusalem, perhaps through a rebuilt Temple.

In my opinion, regardless of what the future holds, we have enough knowledge and information currently to do what is right and to follow the commandments and statutes found in the Hebrew-language based Jewish Scriptures.

Unlike the view promulgated by those who oppose it, the Hebrew-language based Jewish Scriptures, with its codification of laws and statutes, is absolutely **not too hard to follow.**

> **11 For this commandment which I command thee this day, it is not too hard for thee, neither is it far off.**
> **12 It is not in heaven, that thou shouldest say: 'Who shall go up for us to heaven, and bring it unto us, and make us to hear it, that we may do it?'**
> **13 Neither is it beyond the sea, that thou shouldest say: 'Who shall go over the sea for us, and bring it unto us, and make us to hear it, that we may do it?'**
> **14 But the word is very nigh unto thee, in thy mouth, and in thy heart, that thou mayest do it.** [Deuteronomy 30:11-14]

There are some obvious limitations which currently may keep us from following all of the commandments to the letter. As an example, currently sprinkling the *ashes of the Red Heifer* is not done. For the most part, many of us, including myself currently, do not live in the land of Israel. After the last Temple was destroyed in 70 C.E. by Romans, the 'sacrificial system' has been **suspended**. The Christian religion appears to express that it has been 'done away with altogether.'

I would like to mention that while the Israelite people were for seventy years in captivity in Babylon, the sacrificial system was also suspended. That did not mean nor did they ever expect it to mean that it had ended altogether!

There currently is no discernible High Priest, no identifiable male descendant of Aaron, at least that I am aware of.

Obviously, in our current time some of the corporate sacrifices given by Moses cannot be done in like manner as prescribed. However, as a people we should keep the commandments and follow the written Torah (as well as the remaining instructions from the Prophets and Writings) **as best we can do so,** always striving to worship Yehovah in the manner that He chooses!

We would absolutely need to be careful that we **honor Yehovah** in every thing that we do, asking Him for guidance in any undertaking we propose to do. In **"asking Him for guidance,"** that no doubt implies that we, individually, should have a relationship with Him, not only with our own prayer and corporate worship life, but also through the teachings of His written revelation, Hebrew-language based Jewish Scriptures!

Individually, we must love Yehovah with all of our hearts. We must seek His will with all of our being. We must be serious to want to know Him better by regularly reading the written Torah — the Hebrew-language based Jewish Scriptures — with an intention of being experts!

We must love our neighbors as ourselves! In the essence of our lives, we must strive to glorify Yehovah with our every thought, our every action and with our entire being!

To do so is to be the Israel of God!

Jesus Cannot Be The Jewish Messiah*

*If He Ever Took The Authoritative Hebrew-Language Based Jewish Scriptures Out Of Their Plain And Natural Context, Misquoted, Misrepresented, Misappropriated, Contravened Them Or Otherwise Treated Them With Contempt And Disrespect!

Postscript

The book of Matthew actually may have been written in the Hebrew language![82] George Howard found a 14th century manuscript written by Shem-Tob ben-Isaac ben-Shaprut (aka Ibn Shaprut), who wrote a polemic treatise against the Roman Catholic Church persecuting Jews at the time. At the end, he included, in handwritten Hebrew, the book of Matthew. Due to the plethora of Hebrew Idioms not found in the Greek, many believe that version likely went back to an original Hebrew text!

The Lord's Prayer: Hebrew Matthew 6:9-13[83]

⁹ וכן תתפללו אבינו יתקדש שמך

¹⁰ ויתברך מלכותך רצונך יהיה עשוי בשמים ובארץ׃

¹¹ ותתן לחמנו תמידית׃

¹² ומחול לנו חטאתינו כאשר אנחנו מוחלים לחוטאים לנו

¹³ ואל תביאנו לידי נסיון ושמרינו מכל רע אמן׃

⁹ And thus you shall pray: Our father, may your name be sanctified;

¹⁰ and may your kingdom be blessed; may your will be done in heaven and on earth.

¹¹ Give us our bread continually.

¹² Forgive us our sins as we forgive those who sin against us,

¹³ and do not bring us into the hands of a test and protect us from all evil, amen.

I end with Isaiah 53, not found in the weekly Parashah readings!

---

[82] George Howard, 'Hebrew Gospel Of Matthew' (Macon, GA, Mercer University Press).
[83] Hebrew-Matthew 6:13 contains what I consider to be a **Hebrew Idiom,** not found in the Greek Matthew New Testament. It is translated to what I believe is closer to the unvowelled Hebrew: (**"and do not bring us into the hands of a test"** – ואל תביאנו לידי נסיון).

¹ 'Who would have believed our report? And to whom hath the arm of Yehovah been revealed? ² For he shot up right forth as a sapling, and as a root out of a dry ground; he had no form nor comeliness, that we should look upon him, nor beauty that we should delight in him. ³ He was despised, and forsaken of men, a man of pains, and acquainted with disease, and as one from whom men hide their face: he was despised, and we esteemed him not. ⁴ Surely our diseases he did bear, and our pains he carried; whereas we did esteem him stricken, smitten of God, and afflicted. ⁵ But he was wounded because of our transgressions, he was crushed because of our iniquities: the chastisement of our welfare was upon him, and with his stripes we were healed. ⁶ All we like sheep did go astray, we turned every one to his own way; and Yehovah hath made to light on him the iniquity of us all. ⁷ He was oppressed, though he humbled himself and opened not his mouth; as a lamb that is led to the slaughter, and as a sheep that before her shearers is dumb; yea, he opened not his mouth. ⁸ By oppression and judgment he was taken away, and with his generation who did reason? for he was cut off out of the land of the living, for the transgression of my people to whom the stroke was due. ⁹ And they made his grave with the wicked, and with the rich his tomb; although he had done no violence, neither was any deceit in his mouth.' ¹⁰ Yet it pleased Yehovah to crush him by disease; to see if his soul would offer itself in restitution, that he might see his seed, prolong his days, and that the purpose of Yehovah might prosper by his hand: ¹¹ Of the travail of his soul he shall see to the full, even My servant, who by his knowledge did justify the Righteous One to the many, and their iniquities he did bear. ¹² Therefore will I divide him a portion among the great, and he shall divide the spoil with the mighty; because he bared his soul unto death, and was numbered with the transgressors; yet he bore the sin of many, and made intercession for the transgressors.
[Isaiah 53:1-12]